The Heart of the Sun

The Heart of the Sun

This is a book of reflection of a lost time, of memories and growth, and a collection of mind-poems through the knowledge acquired in this school of life.

For more information on 'The Heart of the Sun' and other writings which may be published soon, please visit the website at *http://theheartofthesun. com*

At this website you will find the pictures inside this book, in full color and normal size along with more pictures posted by the author. For your download, you will also find personal articles, poems, power-point files, pdf files, etc. Please use and acknowledge the source. All materials are copyrighted
Please feel free to leave your feedback, comments, suggestions, ideas, and questions for the author Jag B. Mahadeo and he will respond as soon as possible.

The Heart of the Sun

A collection of stories of childhood memories and personal poems based on a young boy's actual experiences in No. 66 Village, Corentyne Berbice, Guyana, South America

Jag B. Mahadeo

authorHOUSE®

AuthorHouse™
1663 Liberty Drive
Bloomington, IN 47403
www.authorhouse.com
Phone: 1-800-839-8640

First published by AuthorHouse   05/27/2011

ISBN: 978-1-4634-1310-1 (sc)
ISBN: 978-1-4634-1309-5 (dj)
ISBN: 978-1-4634-0686-8 (ebk)

Library of Congress Control Number: 2011908217

Printed in the United States of America

"Conventional thinking says that strangers can come together as a family and families could fall apart and then become strangers.
But the Law of Love suggests that we live in a world where there are no strangers. We are all one big family. It's just that some of us have never met.
We are not just the human race.
We are the human family."
Jag B Mahadeo

Guyana—'Land of Many Waters'

The country of **Guyana** is located on the northeastern coast of South America, west of Suriname, north of Brazil, and east of Venezuela.

Georgetown is the capital and principal port.

With an area of 215,000 sq km (83,000 sq mi); Guyana has a population of about 700,000. (Estimate) Approximately 50 percent of the people are of East Indian descent, with about 30 percent of African decent.

Guyana is a country of exceptional natural beauty, a splendid combination of the Caribbean and South America, with fascinating reminders of a sometimes-turbulent past. Perched on the northeast corner of the South American continent, beautiful Guyana stretches 450 miles from its long Atlantic coastline into the dense equatorial forest and the broad savannahs of the Rupununi.

Kaieteur Falls

Located in central Guyana, in the Potaro-Siparuni region is Kaieteur Falls, a Jewel of Guyana. It is a high-volume waterfall on the Potaro River and is the largest single drop waterfall in the world. From its plunge over a sandstone and conglomerate cliff to the first break, it measures 226 meters (741 ft). It then flows over a series of steep cascades which, when included in the measurements, bring the total height to 251 meters (822 ft).

Kaieteur Falls is about five times higher than the better known Niagara Falls, located on the border of Canada and the United States and approximately twice the height of Victoria Falls located on the border of Zambia and Zimbabwe in Africa.

No 66 Village, Corentyne, Berbice

Located in the Lower Corentyne area, No. 66 is probably the smallest village in Guyana. It is situated on the southwestern corner of the Corentyne coast, eight miles from Corriverton Town, and at the convergence of the Atlantic Ocean and the Corentyne River, which separates Guyana and Suriname.

The Mahadeo family home is located in No. 66 Village and this is where most of the childhood stories in this book took place.

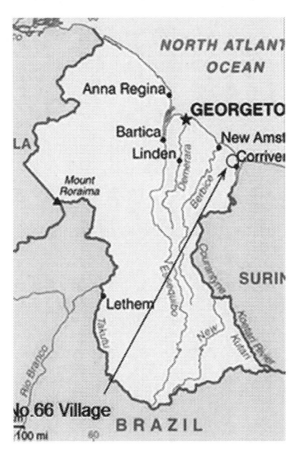

Dedication

With deep love and gratitude in my heart, I dedicate this collection of poems and stories of childhood memories to my Father and Hero, Pandit Budhram Mahadeo 'Papa' and his loving wife and our Mother and inspiration, Rajkumaree Mahadeo 'Mama'.

I thank my brothers Dr. Vishwa Deva B. Mahadeo and Yoganand B. Mahadeo, and sisters Vidya Mahadeo and Vishwanie Mahadeo-Heads for these vivid memories, being an important part of my life, and their part in helping me put together this book. I thank my loving wife Dee, my beloved son Avinash and darling daughter Vashti Devi for their support and understanding during the many hours when my mind was focused on my writings instead of on them. They showed their patience in listening to the many readings and my recollections as I worked on putting together this book. I thank my sister Vidya Mahadeo (Deedee) for her diligent effort in helping to edit my writings in preparation for publishing. Vashti Devi has also been instrumental in helping to edit and organize my thoughts into this book in her one-of-a-kind gentle, loving, kind and humorous way.

Contents

Guyana—'Land of Many Waters' 1

Kaieteur Falls.. 3

No 66 Village, Corentyne, Berbice 5

Dedication 7

Foreword... 13

Introduction.. 15

The Heart of the Sun—Poem... 18

The Village—'Home' 20

The Village Map 27

When the Dogs attacked 28

The House Afire.. 37

The Family Home 40

The Home/Temple—Picture... 44

Free My Mind—Poem 45

Working Out With Papa 46

Pandit Budhram Mahadeo 'Papa'.. 50

Back-dam Adventures.. 56

Rajkumaree Mahadeo 'Mama' 67

Mid-Flight—Poem 70

Celebration of Holi (Phagwah)... 72

Louis Aja.. 77

Mahashay Raghubir Aja 80

Little Boy Knee deep in mud—Poem 83

The Reef Farm 85

Fountain of life—Poem 87

Learning to be a Pandit 89

Body To Mind—Poem 93

Baby Rats 98

My purpose . . . . PLEASE?—Poem.. 103

The Village Master's Roost 107

My Self-Analysis—Poem 109

Playing Cricket with the Gang 111
Of Roses and Thorns—Poem 114
The Raid by GDF Soldiers 116
The Beast in me—Poem 120
Lesson in Discipline 122
2001 The Funeral Pyre—Poem 127
Finding Our Dog Rio 131
Under the Tamarind Tree—Poem 137
Our New Car 138
Out! Out! Out I Say—Poem 142
Buying Contraband 144
Ashes Sown To The Wind—Poem 147
Be Still Dear Heart—Poem 149
Dr. Cheddi Jagan's Visit 150
Meeting the Swan—Poem 154
Sunday Morning At The Beach 157
Rivers Of Blood—Poem 161
Lunging Alligator 162
This Cruel Life—Poem 167
Life . . . What Is It?—Poem 169
The Papaya Medicine Tree 170
Religion! God's Way?—Poem 172
No 68 Primary School 174
Against My Better Judgment—Poem 180
Confusion's End—Poem 182
The Dark Side of Me—Poem 185
Waywardly Meandering-My Mind—Poem 186
Dew Drops—Poem 188
A Tribute 'Mama'—Poem 190
Shafts Of Light—Poem 194
Misery—Poem 196
About the Author 197

On 'Evolution of Mind'

"That I am a better person tomorrow than I am today, better next week than I am this week and better next year than I am this year"
Pandit Budhram Mahadeo

Foreword

In recounting his childhood memories, impressions and reflections in these short stories and poems, Jag Mahadeo paints a vivid picture of the land where he grew up. So much so that the sights, sounds, tastes and smells become real in such a way that, if you too grew up in Guyana, transports you back to a place that you know intimately, but maybe forgot a little. If you didn't grow up in Guyana, they will transport you to a place you believe you know intimately and are just discovering.

These were times when Guyana was stepping out of the shadow of colonial rule into the sunlight—a brave new future. But they were troubled times and many people experienced a physical, political, ideological and spiritual struggle to put Guyana on the map and to aspire to uphold values and traditions—brought with their forbears from far-flung places, such as India, Africa and China-to carve out a new identity which was distinctly Guyanese-not quite Caribbean, not quite Indian, not quite Amerindian, not quite African, but a unique one where all these elements come together.

Jag's family was immersed—even instrumental in this struggle—this rebirth. So much so, that the memories that Jag describes are very potent, albeit personal ones. The ideological, spiritual and moral strength instilled in him by his parents, his family and the community in which he grew up is plain to see. Like so many Guyanese, Jag became one of the wider diaspora who have raised families elsewhere—New York in Jag's case, where the ties to Guyana are strong and his children have a strong sense of identity and indeed, have inherited his values, beliefs and connections to the 'motherland'.

I remember sitting in Jag's back yard in Long Island with his brothers and sisters listening to these stories of the old days-those childhood memories—and it was as if I were there. I remember thinking the stories so interesting from a personal, historical and political perspective that I wished I'd had my video camera with me to record what would have been a unique insight and would have made a wonderful documentary film.

Likewise, I've had the privilege of sitting in the hammock under the old family house in '66', in the dark, with the loud chattering of the crickets and frogs, listening to the stories first hand. I remember chatting with 'Papa' about religion, philosophy, funny family recollections and everything else under the sun and all the family friends that used to visit—either just to check up on Mama and Papa, or to pass a little time playing dominoes on the veranda with the boys and having a laugh and joke.

Mama and Papa were hugely influential figures—not just in their children's lives, but in the community in general and helped shape many futures and indeed, Guyana's enlightenment. I've met three of Guyana's presidents who've called by the house just to pay their respects to Mama and Papa! Mama and Papa became that for me too—I was welcomed into the Mahadeo family as though I was another son and these stories, for me, make my experiences there all the more real and add context to them. I know the places of which Jag speaks. I hear those echoes—those voices. I know the smells, the sounds, the tastes. These stories bring those memories to life in a unique way. These stories hold a poignancy, like the warm breeze in the coconut palms, of a time past but which will live forever through these stories and hold a message for humankind as a whole.

Dr. Richard Heads.
King's College, London

Introduction

In this book of memories and poems, I've taken the opportunity to highlight the lives of a few gentle, spiritual and amazingly gifted personalities, and their influence on my young mind and the minds of other young ones like myself. These great souls were pillars of the community in Guyana, South America especially in the area of Corentyne/Berbice, at a time of much cultural change and political instability. It was desperate a time when people needed guidance and help to survive through the oppressive times brought on by colonialism and later, a dictatorship. Many of us were blessed to have been a part of the lives of these great ones. We were extremely lucky to have experienced their presence and to have been influenced by their tremendous courage and spiritual wisdom. These great souls continue to live on in the thousands of souls who were deeply touched and influenced by them in countless, immeasurable ways.

In this book, I tried to share some of their teachings and accomplishments based on a few of my personal experiences as well as the experiences of others. By doing so, I hope to bring you the reader who knew them, in touch with these characters once again.

For those of you who have not had the pleasure of knowing or interacting with them, I hope to introduce them to you and create a vision of these awesome souls through these writings.

I like to think that these special and unique individuals never really 'pass on' but continue to live on in us and in those who will come after us.

With reverence and total gratitude in my heart for these immortal teachers, these gifts to humanity, I humbly share the memories of my experiences with you the reader, in the hope of reawakening and rekindling the spirit of these personalities within us once again.

I feel privileged that you have ventured on this journey with me by reading this book and sharing in my experiences. I hope that after reading this book, you will have enjoyed meeting Papa, Mama, Mahashay Aja, and Louis Aja and that some of their thoughts and beliefs are, and will be, carried on by you.

My personal stories are centered in the village in which I grew up known as the No. 66 Village. They took place as far back as my memory takes me, from when I was four years old in 1966, to 1978 when I finished High School. The mix of stories and poems are memories of my own childhood or of some experience thus far in my life.

Through the many years when most of these childhood stories took place, and even as I write now, my memories through God's grace are very vivid. They are of fun and impressionable times in my life as a child of that close-knit Guyanese society. I can still smell the smells, hear the sounds, taste the flavors and visualize the sceneries associated with each one of these memories.

The poems, which I have included, are of my own experiences and thoughts, or the feelings which I have experienced through interactions and relationships with others, or as just a passionate student in this Classroom of Life.

I thank God every day for these memories!

Jag

"My whole life is in service to all of mankind"
Pandit Budhram Mahadeo

The Heart of the Sun—Poem

Ejected from the blazing heart of the Sun,
As a burst of energy to the surface
Then as beam of powerful, intense light
left on a journey to the far reaches of outer space

After millions of miles at incredible speed
Through the Earth's atmosphere I slammed into a tree.
I was absorbed into its body and became a tender flower
Of such scent and beauty I attracted a little bee.

It buzzed and danced on my fragrant petals
Then all my precious nectar it slurped in glee.
And left it's tiny, dusty, footprints all over
That started some bizarre changes in me.

Tender petals shriveled and dropped off
And from my stem I grew big and round.
I turned red, soft, and sugary sweet
Then the rain and winds knocked me to the ground.

The soothing rains stopped and after a while
A pretty little girl came wandering by.
Saw me inviting and plump and scooped me up
So very happy she almost started to cry.

She wiped me with soft, dainty little hands
Then sat against the trunk of my parent tree
Smiling, she eyed me over one last time
Then proceeded to eat me delightfully

Now as a part of her little body
In her blood, I flowed through her veins.
Then took up residence inside her head
As a part of her amazing little brain

Now a spark of energy in her life
So far from where my journey had begun.
Here on Earth, as the Light in a Little Girl's eyes
I am still a piece of The Heart of the Sun.

The Village—'Home'

The Village through Jag's eyes (1966-1978)

No. 66 Village, Corentyne, Berbice, Guyana, South America.

To Jagdeep Budhram Mahadeo known to all as 'Jag', this small village was always home.

Compared to other villages in Corentyne, No. 66 Village, located between the '66 Koker' and the '66 Creek', was a very small village. During the years 1966 to 1978 when most of the experiences narrated in this book occurred, the population was approximately 350 residents. It was a wonderful place in which to grow up. The houses were colorful, the fruit trees with dark green leaves were always laden with fruits and the coconut trees swayed tall and graceful in the cool breeze blowing in from the ocean. In Jag's eyes, his village was a vibrant living thing, full of excitement and awe. These were times when a little boy could walk alone in the woods, climb the giant mango trees, play or eat mangoes from the trees as much as he wanted. He could wander off into the woods to search among the 'simitoo' vines and eat the sweet and juicy 'simitoos', or the sweet, purple 'jamoon' freshly picked from the trees. It was a place where a child could spend the afternoon at the ball field watching a game of cricket with only the warning to 'come home in time for dinner' from his parents. The lone 'hill' in the village was a grassy heap of gray dirt about twenty-five feet high by the side of the creek next to the mango trees. This heap was left by an excavator after the dredging of the creek many, many years ago. In the relatively flat land, the children of the village had many adventures climbing the make believe 'mountain' to enjoy the beautiful scenery around. With great pleasure, they would stand or sit at the top and look across the creek in wonder at the thick, green stand of mangrove trees locally known as 'Courida'?

This stand of trees sprouted out of a low, swampy area that was flooded with salt water during every high tide. This was where a few years later, at the age of eighteen, Jag would accidentally lop off his little left toe with his machete while cutting firewood with his mother.

He had arrived home from College for the weekend late Friday evening by hopping a ride on one of the Indian-built Tata buses which were put into service some years ago and still fairly new. On Saturday morning Mama asked him to accompany her to chop some of the mangrove trees to use as firewood in the fire-side—the outdoor wood burning stove—on which she prepared the family meals daily.

They had borrowed a small wooden boat, paddled to this heavily wooded area across the creek and tied the boat to the bushes. This was how the wood will be transported to the road across from his uncle's house. From there they would then have to drag the long trunks to their back yard where they would be cut and split for use with an axe.

Armed with their machetes, with sharp edges specially honed for this task, an axe and pieces of ropes, they trudged through the mud and thick undergrowth of marsh bushes and giant fern-like plants. After locating a stand of suitable sized Courida trees with thick trunks, the two settled down for a day of woodcutting. While he wielded the axe and chopped down the trees, his mother trimmed the small, unusable branches off with her machete. They had a small heap done when Jag cut through the trunk of one particularly tall tree which did not fall down because it was held up to the neighboring tree by some annoyingly strong, brown, rope-like vines.

Taking off his now muddy and slippery sandals, he climbed and shimmied barefooted up this supporting tree to hack away at the offending vines. Sometimes, in situations like this, when Jag worked with his mother, he would tease her by faking injuries and scaring her. This he did today as well. Mama was upset and kept telling him to stop teasing her like that, because something bad could actually happen.

Standing on a firm branch about fifteen feet up, with the strong winds gently swaying the tree, he carefully swung at the vines trying to free the half-fallen tree. As he swung, the wind suddenly picked up, violently shaking the tree and causing him to miss the thick vine. The gleaming blade winked in the sun as it smacked into the limb he was standing on with a dull 'thunk'. He continued on with his task and watched as the tree fell towards the ground, listening as it tore cruelly through the scrubby, green undergrowth on its way down.

Only then, did he notice the bright-red blood pouring out from the stub where his left toe had once protruded. Instead, the small toe was hanging by strands of bloody tissue an inch below his foot and dripping a steady stream of crimson blood into the dark mud below. Calmly he called down to Mama and said "Ma, I just cut off my toe". His mother replied, "stop saying things like that" then as she looked up and saw the blood, she ran close to the tree and pleaded with him to climb down slowly. She watched anxiously as he slowly dropped his machete to the ground, cupped the separated toe close to his foot with one hand to keep it from falling away, and carefully swung down one branch at a time with the other hand.

Finally he sat down on the soft, muddy ground. His mother helped him to tear the inside lining off his shirt, and together with a few pieces from her own clothing, she bandaged the toe in place while keeping the mud that seemed to cover everything from contaminating the wound. She then cut a makeshift crutch for him and together they made their way slowly through the woods to the main road about a mile away where they flagged down a taxi. The driver who stopped turned out to be a familiar face, his uncle Bacchie who became very concerned and quickly drove the two to the Skeldon Hospital. At first the Doctor did not want to reattach the severed toe but his mother insisted, knowing how fast Jag healed. He finally gave in and had the toe sewn back in place by a nurse who turned out to be a cousin of Jag's.

As it turned out, not only was the small toe cut off but half of the one next to it was cut through as well. For the rest of that day and all of the next day, Jag rested under his mother's vigilant care then left for college at 5am on Monday morning.

For the next two weeks he attended classes with his left foot laced onto the outside of his sneaker. As usual he healed very quickly. Within two weeks of using his home remedy on the wounds which consisted of coconut oil and the leaf known as the 'hassa leaf', which his mother insisted that he took with him wherever he went, both toes was completely healed!

In those days one parent's child was the entire village's child and all the people of the village was considered and acted as 'family' to each other. Most children referred to adults other than their parents as their uncles or aunts, even though they may not be related at all.

The village had a single two-lane main road running somewhat north south through the middle of the village. Colorful single and two storey houses, each with its own 'bottom-house' and the mandatory rice-bag hummock, lined this main road on the east and west flanks a mere twenty to thirty feet away from the road and sometimes much closer. Separating the road from the houses on both sides was a shallow drainage ditch referred to as a 'trench' which drained into the creek known as the 66 Creek then out to the Atlantic Ocean. Because of this, the entry into each yard was over some type of a bridge. There were two small stores that sold a mix of everyday amenities ranging from grocery items for the kitchen to hardware and parts for bicycles. There was also one 'rum-shop' where those who chose this type of celebration in the evenings willingly ventured their sanity and intelligence. In front of most of the houses in the village, were small flower gardens which the families tended with pride. Here they planted all types of colorful and fragrant flowers which lit up the front yards with a cheery, friendly, and welcoming atmosphere.

A second street, behind the first row of houses ran parallel to the main road on both sides. These secondary streets were surfaced with sharp red bricks, which were made by burning clay in a huge bonfire. These streets were connected to the main road by cross streets. (See village map)

On the eastern side secondary street, there were eleven houses, also with the flowering plants lining the front fences. Behind these houses, hidden by towering mangrove trees, wild palms, and thick bushes, the 66 Creek and the 'Koker' converged as if in secret, before meandering out as one to where the Corentyne River meet the Atlantic Ocean.

On this 'back' street lived Somesh, a second cousin to Mama. He belonged to the young and energetic group of youngsters under Buddy's leadership who jokingly called themselves the 'gang'. This group of youths was an honest, fun-loving bunch who was very close to Buddy. Jag and Somesh went to Tagore Memorial High School together. They rode their bikes to school and when one was injured, the other took him to school on his bike. Since it seemed that the two took turns getting injured in the strangest of ways, living in the same village was very convenient for them.

On the northeastern end of the village, next to the connecting street, was a Christian Church. Between this structure and the 'Koker' was the tamarind tree where, according to local legend of those who believed in spirits, the 'village master' dwelled. His other dwelling place was supposedly in another tamarind tree which grew on Pandit Mahadeo's property. This huge tree was ten feet from his house, and at about fifty feet tall, was way higher than the third floor tower of the house.

On the western secondary street, there were four houses. This street was also connected to the main road by cross streets. Behind these houses was the popular No. 66 Village Cricket field which was not only the ball field, but the wrestling mat, the volleyball court, the 'kabadi', and the 'coco' grounds, the jogging field, and the boxing gym. It was also the racetrack for the Mahadeo boys, the village children and Buddy's group of boys. This was the playground for all the neighborhood children and the site for the occasional fund-raising 'fair' for churches and political parties.

Beyond this ball-field separated by a hedge of thorny, triangular-stemmed cactus was the 'Budhan' ranch which was chock full of huge mango trees, 'jamoon' trees and all types of bushes and vines. The sweet yellow-red mango fruits and sweet-tart grape-like 'jamoon' tempted all the village children, but the owners of this huge area of fruit trees did not encourage the children to enjoy these fruits. Instead much of the fruits were allowed to rot and go to waste. However, many of the children including Jag, always found a way to eat their 'share' of the fruits before they went to waste.

In this ranch about a stone's throw away from the border of thorny cactus, was a ten to fifteen feet deep pit where in the late 1960's and early 1970's, the red sand was excavated, loaded in dump trucks and used to create the bed of the new main roadway. Over the next few years after its formation, this fresh pit collected clear rainwater, which because of its shallow depth became very warm basking under the tropical sun. The village children enjoyed this pit as the local in-ground pool for many years until it finally became over run by the encroaching tall weeds and water grasses.

To the north of the ball field was the No. 66 Village cemetery. In the center was a low twenty by forty feet shed under which all the cricket players and spectators would take refuge from the hard downpour of rain that occasional interrupted their exciting games of cricket.

To the south was the 66 Village Hindu Mandir (Temple) beyond which was an open area stretching all the way to the 66 Creek which was overrun by the tenacious carrion-crow bush. This weed grew four to seven feet tall and is normally found growing in every open area and sported bunches of finger-like yellow flowers which are quite pungent and distasteful. (picture)

Each day, as the sun rose higher in the sky and the noon-time heat of the day grew uncomfortable, an older man on a bicycle with a cooler attached over the front wheel sold popsicles and ice-blocks made out of sugar, milk, and various seasonings. These made for an inexpensive yet tasty treat for the village children. He was one of the few who had a kerosene-powered refrigerator to make ice. Another man bought blocks of ice from the ice-truck which supplied huge blocks of ice to businesses. From these blocks he scooped ice shavings with a homemade tool and sold this 'crushed' or 'shaved ice' topped with sugary syrup and condensed milk to the children. These men would ride by slowly, blowing on their shrill whistles and ringing their bells to announce their presence, which then prompted the little children to plead to their sympathetic mothers for the 10 cents or 25 cents for an icy treat.

At the time there was no electricity except for the neighbor's personal diesel powered generator which hummed and vibrated every night until around 10 pm. There were no televisions, few radios and no telephones in this area. There were also no ready-made toys available for parents to buy for their children.

In those days children improvised and made their own toys like the 'tagareel'—a rubber-band powered tractor which was fun to play with in the sand and mud, toy boats and various toy weapons.

The tagareel was made from the wooden spools left after a spool of cotton thread was used up in the sewing machines owned by many families. Rubber bands for toys like these were made by cutting the used black inner tubes from the bicycle wheels. Boats were made of soft wood and the spongy 'moko-moko' plant. These were also powered by rubber bands. Precarious-looking scooters were made with hard-to-get steel bearings as wheels. These were fitted on axles whittled from different hardwoods. The containers, which once held powdered milk, were used to make tin-can wheeled rollers. There was also the ever-present slingshot in every little boy's arsenal. These were made out of any strong crotch of a guava tree or any other tree with strong branches. A piece of leather from an old shoe and long strips of rubber cut from an old inner tube completed the sling shot. This device, which was more of a weapon than a toy, was always accompanied by a bag or pocketful of gray, half-inch shots perfectly rounded out of the putty-like clay by hand and dried in the sun until they were rock hard.

Electricity was made available to this entire area of the country in July 1979 after which television sets were slowly introduced. Since there were no local TV stations, the only over-the-air receptions were from the neighboring countries of Suriname and Brazil. These grainy, poor quality receptions still amazed the few who were fortunate to receive them on their new-fangled televisions.

These childhood times were simple, yet fun in a part of the world where all were family and every child respectfully referred to every adult as their uncle or aunt. It is a time and atmosphere which exists no more.

For Jag, this was living in heaven in every way heaven could be described.

The Village Map

No. 66 Village, Corentyne, Berbice, Guyana. South America

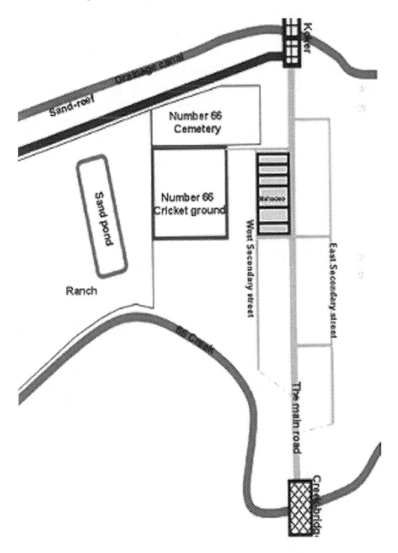

When the Dogs attacked

As he started quickly across the road, the distinct sound of rushing, padded feet on the blacktop sent a shiver of fear up his spine. He turned around just in time to see the moving flashes of the two black and white dogs as they pounced upon him, knocking him down onto his back on the hard, unforgiving, black-top of the road surface.

An hour ago he had just gotten out of bed, woken up by his mother's call. It was a refreshing and beautiful morning with clear blue skies. The remnants of the night dew still hung thick in the air, coating the leaves and grass as a whitish hue and made for a cool, comfortable, feel-good morning. Through the swaying coconut fronds across the road the suns yellow rays split into several swords of light that fenced each other playfully in the safety of their 'bottom-house', the interactive, play area under the front of the house.

The two little black birds that lived in the rafters over the bottom-house performed their drawn out chirp-chirp and flew in lazy circles, following each other back and forth as if trailing some invisible line drawn in the air. Off to the right a half dozen Kiskadees preened themselves in the tender lower branches of the huge high-as-the-house tamarind tree while happily taking turns singing the morning notes of their distinct and musical 'kiss-ka-dee-kis-kis-ka-dee' song.

It was Saturday morning and Jag's mother called on him at 6 o'clock to wash up and take breakfast. He looked forward to his sugar roti (flat bread) in the morning. It was roti cooked with a filling of brown sugar, which melted into a thick, golden-brown delicious syrup trapped and flowing around in the hollow dough of the roti. He sat on the long bench at the kitchen table, his back resting against the cool, light blue painted concrete wall, and enjoyed his sugar roti with tea as Mama continued to prepare breakfast for the rest of the family.

Their nameless black cat who a few days ago had given birth to a noisy litter of kittens in the storeroom under the stairs, stopped preening her babies to come and rub against his leg in anticipation of a piece of roti. Jag enjoyed petting the cat and always laughed excitedly when in response to being rubbed; she would raise her hindquarters off the ground and almost flirtatiously contort her body for more attention. He played with her on the bench for a while then took up his breakfast and quietly stole into the storeroom. Here he opened the window so that he can play with the kittens whose eyes had not yet opened. They were so cute, warm and cuddly-soft and the black mother cat sat back and watched him suspiciously as he picked up each baby in turn and examined them. After he was done satisfying his curiosity, he left them scurrying over each other trying to find a good spot in which to suckle breakfast from their mother.

Jag drained his teacup and dumped his dirty metal plate and cup into the kitchen sink with a loud 'clang'. Pleased with his favorite breakfast, he went out into the front yard, opened the steel gate which his mother had unlocked at daybreak and stepped out onto the wooden bridge spanning the ditch which separated the road from the yard. Here he squatted at the corner of the bridge and marveled at the little gray crabs scurrying up the muddy banks of the shallow ditch, seemingly busy doing something mysterious which he figured only made sense to crabs. Then looking up to the south, he spotted a few ripe guavas shining brightly yellow through the green foliage of the guava tree. This tree grew hanging over the ditch which was outside of the yard and he quickly ran over to pick and eat the delicious beauties before any other early morning passersby, took advantage of them. These guava fruits were so sweet and deep red on the inside that the redness showed through the bright yellow skin. The birds always got to them first and it was a rare treat when anyone got the opportunity to enjoy a whole ripe guava.

His task this morning was to walk to his Chacha's (Uncle) house, which was almost at the south end of the village next to the 'creek-bridge' and pick up from his Chachee (Aunt) the little tomato and bigan (eggplant) plants which his mother had requested a few days ago. The past week was very rainy and wet and Mama knew that this weather presented the perfect opportunity to transplant the tender, young plants into the freshly prepared soil in the 'back-dam' vegetable garden which was located on the creek-dam, about four miles inland. Whenever they planted tiny seedlings at the farm in this damp and cool weather, they did not have to go through the task of building the small leaf-covered structures, which protected the seedlings from the blazing hot sun.

The two ferocious, mottled black and white guard dogs that constantly terrified the neighborhood children were chasing each other, playing catch-the-tail and barking loudly in their well-fenced-in yard of the little white house across the road. Every morning these dogs would complain to the whole village as an old black man walked by. This old man worked at the government compound by the creek bridge and as he walked by, he whistled in a high-pitched note while spinning his walking stick in his hand. The little boy called him the 'whistling man' and listened to him in envy. He could not whistle and every time he heard this man, it prompted his renewed but futile efforts that sometimes ended with his mouth sore from his fruitless practicing. He was the only one among his brothers and sisters who could not whistle, something he will never be able to do.

This morning the two dogs barked wildly at Jag as he walked past the house. He dashed by the next two houses in fear as the two fixed their attention on him, standing on their hind legs, pawing wildly at the white picket fence in anger while their shrill barking echoed loudly in his ears.

The small village was slowly coming to life and someone turned on a radio tuned in to the radio station known as 'Nickerie'. This station transmitted from the area known by the same name, in the neighboring country of Suriname. This very popular radio station played beautiful Indian movie songs all day and could be heard playing at all hours throughout the village. This station was largely responsible for helping to instill the Indian music and culture in the majority Indian population of this part of Guyana.

It was Saturday, the biggest and busiest day at the Skeldon Market which was about eight miles away. Taxis and noisy open topped trucks drove past on the road, heavily laden with the farmers crops destined for the market. Villagers, dressed in colorful clothes, waited at the side of the road trying to flag down a taxi for this very important weekly market trip. On Saturdays most of the villagers stocked up their kitchens for the entire week. Most people also saw Saturdays as an opportunity to socialize at the market. It was a popular meeting place for the older children and teens. There they could spend the day enjoying the wide variety of locally made treats such as the 'gulaab jamoon', 'sugarcake' and 'jalabi', as well as the tasty and succulent tropical fruits. In this atmosphere of the mixed, open-air vegetable market and covered stalls, dozens of teenagers participated in the social interactive games, and courting rituals that all teenagers seemed to enjoy playing.

A few hire cars 'taxis' swerved dangerously around two bold donkeys prancing carelessly in the middle of the road, their muscular necks dipping in rhythm to their dancing steps, so Jag moved to the grassy edge of the road. When he saw no more cars approaching, he ran yelling and waving at the two wayward, four-legged traffic hazards to chase them off the road and into the side streets. Seeing the small screaming boy approaching, with arms waving insanely, the donkeys stopped, stared, brayed at him in defiance, and then took off at a gallop in the direction of the cricket ground with the boy still running and whooping behind them. Jag had seen the occasional vehicular accident involving animals on the road and many of these were very serious. He did not want to see another one today.

After the brief activity of chasing the brazen donkeys, the boy finally arrived at his destination slightly out of breath. His Chacha was already awake and was adding water to the radiator of his farm tractor in preparation for a long day at the rice fields. He walked into the yard and greeted his uncle with the usual "Namaste Chacha". His Chacha answered in kind, and while his Chachee went into the backyard to get the plants, he chatted with his uncle. In response to his query, his uncle told him that Prakash, his eldest son was having his breakfast in preparation for the 'backdam' trip and Satish, the second son, had ridden his bicycle to the next village, which was his normal morning routine.

His Chacha was stocky, powerfully built and always walked like a man with a mission, head upright, shoulders back, and with a deliberate stride. His relationship with his Chacha was a very special one. On his daily walks past his home, if his uncle saw him looking a bit sad or dejected, he always made the time to stop and find out if everything was okay. Because of this caring attitude, Jag thought very highly of his uncle. He always enjoyed talking with his uncle and loved that his uncle treated him almost like an adult. He seemed to always know when Jag was in trouble and always sought to discuss, clarify and explain things away in his very unique and emphatic way.

Within a few minutes his aunt came back carrying the plants with the lower roots carefully wrapped in a few sheets of wet newspapers. After bidding them a farewell 'Namaste', (A Hindu greeting paying homage to the divinity in each other) he left for home with the precious plants. Once out on the street he paused by the side of the road to look in interest as two of the Sugar Estate trucks tried to navigate through the narrow

Number 66 Bridge. This structure was a rectangular truss type steel bridge constructed with huge white-painted steel beams which straddled the fast flowing Number 66 Creek. At about fifty feet long, its steel structure was imposing in its size and uniqueness. It is a well-known structure in the Corentyne area and is said to be the only bridge of the type ever built with all steel. Beneath the bridge the tea colored water rushing from the savannahs four miles inland went on to empty into the Corentyne River and then the Atlantic Ocean.

Jag headed home with the delicate package of tender plants firmly held in his hand. He loved the pungent aroma of the tomato plants and squished a few leaves between his fingers to release more of the sweet smell. As he walked home trying to imitate his uncle's walk, he listened in pure envy to the loud whistling of the 'whistling man' who was by the koker, (picture) at the other end of the village. He tried again and again to whistle but only succeeded in getting dirt from the plants into his mouth.

The koker marked the end of the village to the north and here the water rushing through the koker gates twisted past the houses on the last street to the east. The bushy area behind the houses on this back street was a mysterious place where many of the wildlife in the area still lived. Beyond the four-foot high levee that protected the villages from the high tides, the area was thickly forested by mangrove trees, which the locals called 'Courida' and a mix of thorny briars, ferns and other salt-water-loving bushes. Here in the secret hideaway of the thick green woods, the 66 Creek and the Koker canal converged, then continued on their way for approximately another quarter mile, before emptying into the mouth of the wide Corentyne River.

The dozens of twenty to thirty foot long fishing boats in the neighboring villages, which plied the Corentyne River and braved the Atlantic Ocean for their daily haul of fish, called the areas next to the structures of the koker and the creek bridge their home. (picture)

Here these small wooden fishing boats came in to transfer their catch of fish onto the large trucks to be transported to the markets. This was also where hundreds of unwanted bony fishes and sharks were left stranded daily, only to writhe in agony and die a horrible death after being tortured by the fishing nets for hours. Eventually their lifeless, fly ridden carcasses were washed back to always-welcoming sea by the next receding high tide.

The creek and koker canals were also indispensable to farmers when, during the rice planting season, the trail leading to the fields became too torn up by the tractors and way too muddy to be traveled. Supplies for the rice fields where then taken in by boat, and boatloads of vegetables were brought back home from the vegetable gardens inland

Now almost home, the young boy looked left then right, as he was taught to do, before crossing the road. All was clear and he started across the road when he heard a rush of padded feet. Turning around just in time, he saw the two big, black and white dogs as they charging towards him. Before he knew it the first one bowled him over hard into the unforgiving, rough asphalt. Raising his hands to cover his face against the attack, he screamed, flailed, and kicked wildly as the big dogs had their way with him. While one dog chomped down on his right leg and shook him like a ragdoll, the other tore at his short pants around his bottom, the long, sharp teeth plunging deeply into the boy's flesh. The attack continued for what seemed to him like an eternity, until finally the 'whistling man' ran over, dropped his shoulder bag and started hitting and pushing the dogs off with his walking stick. He then stood guard over the boy, brandishing his stick while the dogs' owner, an old lady, struggled to control the vicious, snarling dogs.

His savior used his stick to keep the dogs at bay while his Mama and Nanee, (Grandmother) hearing the screams and seeing the commotion, came running out of the house. His mother gently picked him up and carried him home. Blood was streaming from his scalp which was gashed open against the blacktop when he fell and was pouring out of his right thigh, right leg and his bottom where his pants were almost shredded off of his small body. His Nanee and Mama cleaned him up carefully, bandaged his wounds as best as they could and after dressing him in clean clothes, Mama flagged down a taxi to take him to the doctor.

The young boy was crying and sniffling non-stop. He was in a lot of pain and bleeding all over waiting room, which prompted the doctor to look after him immediately. Upon examining his many wounds, the doctor removed from his right lower leg a long canine tooth, which had broken off in the boy's leg. He then gave him a tetanus shot, bandaged his wounds and sent him home for the day with his caring parents.

The next day his Nanee approached the owner of the dog to get a snip of the dogs' hair to prepare the hair-of-the-dog treatment for Jag's many injuries. This ancient remedy is supposed to prevent infections of the wound. Some of the dog's hair was clipped off and mixed in coconut oil and this concoction was used on the wounds to help in the healing process.

Amazingly, it worked and a short time later young Jag was back to being his mama's little helper again.

"All of my relationships in this life have been that of a student and teacher, in which I have always been, and always will be, the student"

Jag B Mahadeo

The House Afire

He stood frozen on the spot in shock, feet splayed wide in the drains separating the spinach beds and stared in horror at the angry, red flames attempting to follow the black, oozing smoke up the concrete wall in an attempt to attack and engulf the white-painted wooden structure of the house above.

The little boy had a dangerous obsession. He was fascinated with fire and always asked his mother if he could strike the matches to light the fire in the 'fireside' (picture) upon which she prepared the family meals. Whenever he could, he would steal the matches and sneak away to the open backyard to set fire to whatever little dried grasses and leaves he could find or to the drying heap of household and yard refuse.

On the lower right side of the house there was a concrete wall that held a window, but no room in the back. (For a planned extension that did not happen) Behind this wall was strewn a heap of coarse white sand about four feet deep and ten feet wide, which was left over from past constructions around the house. Away from the house and lining the picket fence were a few beds of spinach which his mother tended, and next to these beds stood a fifteen feet high 'sijan' tree, (also known as drumsticks) This tree bore a stick-like vegetable that was used to prepare a delicious curry. The leaves were also use to prepare a spinach-like delicacy that all the children enjoyed immensely for its unique taste.

On this heap of coarse sand, the children found the perfect play area on which to use their home made toys like the 'tagareel'. The tagareel is a rubber-band powered device made from the wooden spools left over, after a spool of cotton thread was used up. The 'rubber bands', which ran through the center of the spool, were cut from inner tubes of bicycle tires which were no longer usable. A sliver of wax from a candle kept the wound up rubber band lubricated so that it unwound and rolled freely against the stick used to wind it up. On the two ends of the spool Jag used a razorblade to notch and gave traction to the wheels which helped it to climb up the sand and dirt. The large grained, white sand was mixed in with leaves, papers and other debris which the brisk, eddying wind released behind the wall.

The loose white sand was easy to dig and move around and here he had a lot of fun trying to playfully bury his squirming dog Rio. After lying obediently in the sand for a while, the dog would suddenly jump up, violently shake the sand off his body, and run off with the squealing little boy chasing him all over the yard. There was an old car tire, half buried in the sand, which he sometimes used to roll around the yard, pretending that he was driving his own little car.

One day on an uncontrollable whim, he separated and gathered all the flammable stuff which he could find mixed in with the sand, brought in some old newspapers to add to the pile and stacked them all together with the old tire leaning against the blue-green painted concrete wall. He then went to the kitchen, stole the matches while his mother was not looking, ran back and gleefully struck one to the waiting pile of debris. The innocent-looking, tiny yellow flame licked hungrily at the inviting stack of papers. He sat close and watched excitedly as the papers slowly burned and as the small flame spread and grew wide. He moved a step back as the heat grew in intensity. Within a few minutes however, his glee turned into pure horror as the old rubber tire within the stack caught fire and quickly started to burn, with thick, black smoke curling high up the concrete walls as if beckoning and teasing the angry, red flames down below to follow. The red flames way up high and now making an evil, roaring, hissing noise, scared him and he slowly backed away. Helplessly, he now stood transfixed and paralyzed in fear. He could not think straight and did not know what to do.

From behind him someone started screaming, and after a few long moments, the persistent yelling slowly registered in his mind. It was his neighbor's wife, known to everyone as Sema. She was screaming at the top of her voice that 'the boy has set fire to the house! the boy has set fire to the house!' Her voice, heard often enough when she usually summoned her children home, was very loud and piercing and she kept repeating her 'alarm' as she approached the fence, trying to get the attention of anyone who can help.

Jag's father and mother heard the racket, smelled the smoke, ran around the house together and stopped in shock. Then realizing the impending disaster, they lost no time in rushing buckets of water from the conveniently open, lower concrete water tank and splashing it on the angry flames. Time seemed to stand still as the flames finally receded in defeat and slowly died. As if in defiance, it left the evidence of its passing as a huge swath of black, oily stain on the once clean, painted concrete wall which marked the wall for years to come. The heavy smoke which was now thinning and mixed with steam, settled over everything as dusty black soot.

With the situation finally under control, the attention of everyone now turned to the still-paralyzed little boy standing between the beds of spinach. Deservingly, he had his bottom spanked and in the next few days withstood many of those feared lectures from his Papa.

The Family Home

The big house was painted white and greenish-blue with a reddish-pink color on its veranda's trim and railings. As was most of the houses around, it was topped off with a red painted metal roof. The house stood almost at the center of the small No. 66 Village on the western flank of the wide two-lane road, and faced the rising sun. This uplifting location was a perfect fit for the deeply religious family. Pandit Mahadeo (Papa) and his entire family believed in rising early in the mornings and doing their morning prayers facing the brilliance of the sun in all its glory.

The concrete and wooden house was built by Papa himself with the help of a crew of carpenters in the late 1950's. The house was extended around 1967 into the present size by adding on the veranda with its entrance stairway, library room and a few other rooms on the left side of the building.

The property was somewhat larger than most in the village and was surrounded with a wooden fence. In the front yard to the left, a coconut tree spread its wide fronds next to the drainage ditch bordering the road. On the inside of the fence a bushy 'balambi' tree snaked up and over the drain flowing from the back of the yard. The green balambi fruit was very tart and acidic and was enjoyed by the children who dipped it in a mixture of salt and pepper before eating it. It was also used to make very delicious chutney with pepper and vinegar, which the family enjoyed with their meals.

Immediately in front of the house was a long, narrow flowerbed which always displayed a beautiful mix of flowers. In the center of the flowerbed was a small hibiscus plant sprouting big, bright-red flowers and reaching around it were white roses blooming in huge clumps at the ends its thorny stalks. Around these were scattered sunflowers, marigold, cattails, 'coxcombs', and lady-slippers. All of these plants seem to spring out of a mat of delicate red and white 'jump-and-kiss' flowers, which hugged and covered the grayish sandy soil. This was the most fertile spot in the yard since many years before, Pandit Mahadeo used to keep his milking cow tethered to this area of the front fence each morning when he brought her home to be milked. Here the foliage and flowers bloomed in splendor.

The bridge leading from the road into the yard was made of two inch thick by ten inch wide greenheart planks and upon these were nailed small strips of wood which aided the little sky-blue Minor Morris in getting up the wet, slippery bridge on the frequent rainy days. The gate was made of welded galvanized pipe frame and chain-link type grating. It was locked at night by wrapping a two inch thick steel chain around the center poles and fastening the ends with a brass padlock.

In this hot climate, the outdoors was enjoyed at the 'bottom-house'. These common outdoors family areas were usually located underneath a portion of the second floor of the house. Since it was open all around except in one direction, it was breezy and cool. Every 'bottom-house' had at least one hummock usually made out of a converted 'rice bag'.

The Mahadeo's 'bottom-house' was quite spacious and Papa usually parked his car in the front half of the area. He parked it on top of a ten feet circular patch of cement which was the remnants of the cement which was mixed on that spot when the house was first built many years ago. The car was parked facing the stairway going up into the veranda and on the right of the car a comfortable 'rice bag' hummock was strung between the two upright blue-green painted green-heart (a strong tropical wood) columns. A quarter of the 'bottom-house' space was taken up by six, eight-foot long, two feet wide tables and matching benches, which, together with the large blackboard, comprised of the classroom of the Hindi/English school, run by Papa and Mama. Entering the yard from the road, there was a patch of grass about fifteen feet wide by forty feet deep through which two almost invisible ribbons of wheel tracks showed. This patch of green grass was kept trimmed short by the three Mahadeo boys Buddy, Jag and Yog.

The first floor was made of concrete and consisted of two large rooms with solid wooden windows which opened outwards, and a small enclosed shower. The room to the left was the large kitchen with a two burner clay 'fireside'. To the right was the visitor/meeting room/sitting room area.

The second floor was made of all wood and comprised of four bedrooms, a large living room area and the veranda. The front of the house on the second floor had all glass windows that allowed the swift breezes coming off the ocean to cool the house on very hot, muggy days.

The third floor was a single room known to all as the 'tower' and was the family temple and prayer room where the family performed all their daily prayers and celebrations of birthdays and other special occasions.

Behind the house was a concrete water tank about eight feet square and six feet deep that contained cool, clear and refreshing water. This tank was mostly in-ground with about thirty inches above ground level. It was cleaned out and dried about once a year and while this was being done, the large three feet square opening was usually covered by a loose tarp instead of the large and heavy concrete cover. Once, when the tank was empty Jag's sister Shanie, fell into the tank when she accidentally stepped onto the tarp. Her grandmother, who they all called 'Nanee', was washing clothes on the concrete slab about eight feet away. Shanie who her siblings called 'Lil' was hanging the clothes out to dry while singing of her favorite Indian song titled 'Surangani'. Unwittingly, she stepped on the tarp that covered the opening and fell into the tank. Nanee at first thought that Lil had pulled some kind of disappearing trick on her and was shocked when, surprisingly, she pulled herself out of the tank completed unscathed. This was, and still is a running joke among the now grown Mahadeo children.

The huge volume of water held in this tank usually supplied the entire community with clean drinking water during the frequent times when the public well or running water system failed. At these times of water emergency, families from the entire village and several neighboring villages came daily with their buckets to carry water home for drinking and cooking. Straddling this huge tank, a sturdy wooden structure made of thick greenheart timber columns rose about thirty feet high and supported a big steel water tank which supplied the entire house with running water.

Encroaching into the timberworks of the tanks, the reaching gray-brown limbs of the nearby breadfruit tree spread out in all directions and competed for height with the steel tank to the right. The slender, yet strong branches supported the huge green leaves, finger-like flowers, and the heavy, lime-green globes of breadfruits. (picture)

Behind the giant breadfruit tree was a row of fruit trees. There was a 'spice' mango tree, a red guava tree and a white guava tree. To the left were three huge, bushy cherry trees and to the extreme right was a 'byre' tree which produced these one inch round spongy fruits with a hard, rough seed. In between these were Mama's vegetable garden beds.

Against the picket fence on the left was an old calabash tree. This tree bore large gourd fruits, which all the children learned how to split open using a saw and made bowls that were used in the kitchen.

Ringing the back yard were seven coconut trees which supplied the family with enough coconuts to make cooking oil and the occasional treat of a young 'water' coconut for the children.

Three parallel drains were dug to collect water to quench the thirst of the plants in the dry season and to drain the beds of vegetables in the rainy season. From these muddy ditches sprung spongy stems which supported lush, dark green, dinner-plate-sized leaves of eddoes, an elephant ear plant which produced edible leaves and tubers. In this miniature tropical haven, dozens of species of fishes, some of which grew up to eight inches long, crabs and large snails found home. This was also the 'pond' where the children sent their little boats made out of foam or soft wood on imaginary trips to faraway places.

This was the 'playground' where the Mahadeo children played hide-and-go-seek, climbed trees and played other childhood games.

This was and still is, the 'Mahadeo family home'.

The Home/Temple—Picture

Free My Mind—Poem

Free my mind from
Numerous tethers of mighty stones.
Help me hold my head up
Above the raging, crashing waves.
Let me force a smile
upon my dry, trembling lips,
and look way past
my sad, cloudy and dreary days.

Help me see beyond just
the beauty of the sparkling sun,
and leave my terrible nightmares
in the bed in which they lay.
Share the smile that I force upon my lips
and check my mammoth ego at the gate.

Let me cast my distinct shadow
even in the dark.
Leave my deep lasting tracks
in the clay of the earth.
Help me rise far above the rigors
that misery spawns
and not whet my insatiable appetite
toward a futile, speedy end.

Working Out With Papa

It was five in the morning when his eyes opened to his father's low call. The twelve year old answered "Yes Pa" and got up slowly, listening to his father's fumbling in his bedroom as he got dressed. Moving with care in the dark, trying to be quiet so as not to disturb the others who were still asleep, Jag slowly pulled his clothes on, rubbed his eyes and headed downstairs to untie the rigged up 'alarm system' from around his father's car. This was a 1966 light sky-blue Morris Minor (picture) with the license plate PW278 which he loved to wash and keep clean for his father. As he always did every morning when he took down the rigging, he lightly caressed a small, crumbled dent the size of his fist, on the topside of the left rear fender which was caused by a collision with the blade of a caterpillar grader which was working on building the road some years ago. This was the only blemish in the otherwise perfect form of this much-loved car and little Jag saw this as a battle scar that showed the power and strength of this beautiful little car versus the goliath of the caterpillar tractor.

It was a beautiful, cloudless morning and the clear, star-studded skies stretched like a blanket in all directions except towards the distant south in the direction of the headwaters of the Corentyne River, where the constant flickering lighting seemed to always

jump and play between the ever-present clouds at all hours of the night. Since it was about eight miles away, it was an eerie sight because the expected sound of any accompanying thunder never reached the listening ear.

He then unlocked the brass-colored padlock that secured the steel chain around the wrought iron gate which led into the yard and spacious 'bottom-house' of their seemingly huge two-story house with the quaint small tower. This third floor which was known to all as 'the tower' had glass windows all around. It was dedicated solely as the family temple and prayer room. This is where the members of the family performed their daily 'Sandhya', weekly 'Havan', practiced their meditation and celebrated their birthdays and other family occasions.

At this time of the morning there was no traffic except for the occasional truck known locally as the 'federal'. This truck boasted long, solid, wooden benches and transported the sugarcane workers to the cane fields of the Skelton Estate eight miles away. At the estate the workers labored under the scorching tropical sun, cutting the sugar cane, gathering and tying them into bundles, then carrying the bundles on their backs and loading them into steel 'punts' to be taken to the sugar factory. This sugar estate was the largest employer of people in the area.

Aside from these noisy trucks, the only others that ventured to break the sweet silence of the morning were the roosters whose crescendos of 'cock-a-doodle-doos' hung in the still, early morning air until all had answered each other's enquiring call.

In the middle of this silent, almost traffic-less road the two, father and son, performed their Yoga exercises for the next half hour beginning with breathing exercises and then moving on to more intricate Yoga postures. Papa patiently instructed Jag on the correct posture and length of time for each posture. At a very young age, his son had started to participate in demonstrations of Yoga at conventions, religious, and public gatherings, and Papa was very proud of his pupil. These exercises demanded commitment and patience, and as father and son did their routines they were both careful not to break the silence of the morning with many words. Papa used gestures as much as he could to communicate to his son while coaching him. It was during these early years and peaceful mornings that the young boy learned to value, appreciate and really enjoy the quiet moments of the mornings.

After their Yoga routine, the two took off running to the steel creek-bridge to the south, back north to the koker and then back home. Papa lead the way, with his favorite knotted walking stick in hand to ward off the rare, yet possible dog attack and Jag following closely behind, frequently looking over his shoulder to monitor any following demons of the dark, those ever-present product of his over-active twelve year old imagination. At this hour, it seems that even the village dogs hesitated to destroy the solitude and calm of the morning, for when one made an enquiring call about the two stealthy shadows moving about on the road, he gave up quickly after receiving no answer from his fellow watchdogs.

A few minutes later as the two stood side by side at the 'bottom-house' and finished up with the last set of breathing exercises, the sky began to get lighter as the quickly approaching daylight bullied away the dark blanket of night and the last of the still flickering stars slowly dimmed away.

The soft beauty of the white rose bush straddling the front fence seemed to help light up the day and the alluring scent of the multiple foot long bunches of white roses which bent the flexible limbs down to the ground permeated the calm air. Father and son sat quietly, appreciating the gifts around them and watched as the two blackbirds started their morning routine of feeding their babies.

These calm mornings with his father and hero, were of appreciation, peace, influence and growth, and would eventually help to mold Jag into becoming the responsible adult he would one day become.

On 'Exercising and the body'

"This body is your God's temple. You want to worship God? You want to show God your Love? Show him how you can take care of this Temple, this Gift that he granted to you. Always exercise your body, your mind and put only the right amount of good food in your body."

Pandit Budhram Mahadeo (Papa)

Pandit Budhram Mahadeo 'Papa'

Budhram Mahadeo was born on the 22nd of July 1925 to a deeply religious couple, Mr. Mahadeo Shivdhan, who had emigrated from India and Mrs. Gangia Shivdhan, who was born in Guyana of Indian immigrants.

They were known as Ma and Pa to all had seven children. There were the eldest daughter Hubranie, also known as, Deedee, Budhram known by most as Papa or Bhaiya, Gowrinauth also called Dad and Dos, Bhanmatee, or Gayatree, Lutchmin, known by all as Savitri or Sabi, Indromatee or Asha and Ograsain also known as Baba or Ogra.

Ma and Pa had a house next to the 66 Village Koker, a sluice which opened and closed between tides to drain the water from the farms and rice fields. Here the Mahadeo grandchildren spend many childhood days playing and climbing the numerous guava trees in the back yard, playing hide and seek, and sometimes seeking refuge with their grandmother, whom they all called Ma, when they got into trouble at home for any mischievous behavior.

The three brothers, known to all as Papa or Bhaiya, Daad or Dos, and Baba or Ogra were all of very strong characters and personalities. Their strong-mindedness caused minor internal philosophical clashes among the three, but this also made for each becoming individually and independently stronger as time went by. At a young age Ogra went to study in Russia, (USSR at the time) then a few years after his return had migrated to Canada. Because of this he was, in many ways a stranger to the siblings of his brothers and sisters. Years later he would eventually create a strong and lasting fatherly bond to Jag and his family and they enjoyed many vacations at each other's homes.

Pandit Budhram Mahadeo was married to Rajkumaree and together they had five children, three boys and two girls. They are Vidya, Vishwa Deva, Vishwanie, Jagdeep and Yoganand.

Budhram Mahadeo was a man for the people and his entire life was dedicated to his country, his community and his fellow man. He was the block of granite upon which the foundation of his family rested. He was the block of granite from which his five children were carved. This morally incorruptible man was one of a huge caring heart who saw and held the community and, in his words, 'all of mankind' as his family and treated everyone as part of his family. He was the kind of person who felt and understood the emotions and the heartbeat of the common man. He fought for their welfare by getting involved in every aspect of their lives in which he could be of help and make a difference in their lives. Everyone addressed him as 'Papa', which means father, 'Bhaiya', which means brother, or Pandit which is a Hindu Priest, and in everyone he left a distinct impression of patience, love, caring, and empathy. He lived the example of the perfect son, brother, father, husband and teacher.

He was a well known and highly respected Arya Samaj Pandit (Hindu Priest). The Arya Samaj is an organization founded by Swami Dayananda on 10th April 1875 to re-establish and promote the teachings of the Vedas—the earliest scriptures in existence and the foundation of Hinduism. Meaning "Noble Society" the Arya Samaj has worked to further female education, opposes a caste system based on birth rather than on merit, opposes untouchability, child marriage, and idolatry. Over the past 136 years the organization has established missions, orphanages, homes for widows and a network of schools and colleges throughout the world. It has undertaken medical work, famine and other forms of relief efforts. The Arya Samaj Movement was in the forefront of the independence struggle in India and members of this organization, where ever they may be, are always found to be in the forefront fighting for democracy and freedom.

Based on his strong belief in the teachings of the Vedas and the goals of the Arya Samaj, Pandit Budhram Mahadeo worked hard to instill the Vedic culture and values in the younger generations. This included, taking the time to teach Hindi and English at his free private school held at his 'bottom-house'. In his absence, his wife, his children or advanced students taught the classes. He encouraged impromptu sessions of philosophical discussions which seemed to arise spontaneously whenever he had a group of people around him—and it did not matter whether it was a political or spiritual gathering, or whether they were adults or children. People of all walks of life would drop in at his home at all hours for these discussions which he always entertained, for he believed that life was all about gaining knowledge and that one can learn from all experiences and from everyone.

He was well known for his honesty and principled actions. In all his years of performing countless Havans (Hindu Religious sermons) and Hindu weddings, when it was normal practice for all other Pandits/priests to accept a substantial fee for their services, Pandit Mahadeo refused any form of payment. He insisted that it was his duty to perform service to his community and he did not take money to even cover the cost of transportation or personal expenses. Sometimes people insisted on paying for the religious services in the form of 'dakshina'. (Donation in gratitude to the Guru as recommended by the scriptures) Usually this payment was in the form of cash, for which Pandit Mahadeo would give a receipt made out as donation to the Mandir/Temple. Sometimes the dakshina was in other material forms such as clothes, etc. These items were taken home and later given by his wife 'Mama' to the less fortunate such as the beggars who showed up daily at his home. Once every month he would sit at his table on the veranda, empty all the envelopes of dakshina money out on the table in a heap and diligently count it and prepare to give it to the Mandir the following Sunday.

A very active, solidly built man, five feet nine inches tall and about one hundred and seventy pounds, Pandit Mahadeo enjoyed being involved with the youths of the surrounding villages in all types of activities, from playing cricket, 'kabadi,' and 'coco' to engaging in political and/ or philosophical discussions with them after a game of cricket. He took advantage of opportunities like these to infuse within them the values and philosophies he held dear to his own heart. This he did in a fun manner which kept the young ones interested in these otherwise boring subjects. He had a giant magnetic personality which drew people of all intellectual levels to him in discussions and debates in topics ranging from the political views and events of the day to ancient Vedic rituals and philosophical commentaries. Papa's oratory skills were so profound and loved by his people that whenever he was present at a function or social gathering he was always asked to contribute by making a speech. Most people regarded it as an honor to have Pandit Mahadeo visit or speak at their house or event.

With an erect posture he walked with confidence in every step and always had a quick endearing smile which made those around him feel calm and comfortable. He was highly respected by his people and sometimes even feared by those of questionable morals. He always stood firm for the principles he believed in against all others. He dedicated his life to the defense and service of his country and community and always insisted that he will protect 'his people at any costs, even with his life if necessary.

This block of granite was immovable in his dedication to others and he lived his life proud of the fact of never having once compromised his values under any circumstances, even during those many times when he was jailed for voicing or fighting for these values.

He shared a vision of freedom for his people with Dr Cheddi Jagan, the founder of the People's Progressive Party, and was an active and dedicated founding member of the party. This vision of freedom coupled with his Vedic upbringing and his deep philosophical views made for a man committed to the cause of reducing suffering and oppression for his people and for the equal rights of all—men and women alike.

After numerous attempts of bribery to win over Pandit Mahadeo to the ruling People's National Congress, (PNC)—a dictatorship installed by the CIA and kept in power by fraudulent means and rigged elections, the government resorted to pressure and harassment. His home and property were raided on a daily and nightly basis with no regard to time or circumstance, to search for 'illegal guns' which were never found. (documented in later stories in this book) On trumped up charges, he and his wife were jailed many times in order to try and subdue his strong will. Over the years every attempt failed miserably. He proved himself to be unbreakable and unshakeable.

As leader of the local and regional PPP groups he went door to door to spread the message of freedom and people power and to encourage the 'common man' to join in the struggle for freedom. He was a rice farmer and represented the country's farmers as the President of the Rice Producers Association or the RPA. In this capacity he helped to resolve as many of their issues as he possibly could. This dedication to his work in helping people took him away from his family for extended periods of time when he went to help farmers in other regions of the country.

His communal work was non-ceasing and people from his community approached him with their political, public, personal and most private of their own problems to which he responded with confidence and ease, and their problems were always kept in confidence. His advice was highly respected by all. Broken families came to him for counseling and he used his tactful leadership and facilitation skills to bring them back together as a stronger family unit. His deep value system which he never compromised were based on his philosophical, yet considerate and kind approach to all his fellow men to whom he dedicated himself to be of service.

One of his teaching was that 'we should be better tomorrow than we are today, better next week than we are this week, and better next year than we are this year'. He lived his teachings, always practiced what he preached, and advanced himself spiritually as well educationally every day of his life.

He was awarded the titles of Shastri and Dharmacharya by the Arya Samaj Movement and in his later years in 1996, was awarded with the Cacique Crown of Honor (CCH), the third highest national award of the country, by the Government of Guyana.

This was Budhram Mahadeo, a man of the people and for the people, Papa, (father) Bhaya, (brother) and Pandit to all and the epitome of strength, discipline, empathy, and love for all his people. Papa said "My duty in this life is service to all mankind" and he spent his entire life perfecting this belief and living these words to the best of his ability.

"I believe in service. My chosen path of life is Service to God, Service to my people and lastly, service to myself.

The self is not important, but when one serves his God and his people, the self is taken care of."

Pandit Budhram Mahadeo (Papa)

Back-dam Adventures

His small, bare feet raw from the hot, sharp edges of dried clay tracks made by the hooves of animals, feet of men and deep threads of farm tractors, the nine year old brown skinned boy plodded on, looking up just enough to see his mother's bare muddy feet walking ahead. He was afraid to look up into the distant line of blue-green haze of trees, four and a half miles away that marked their destination. Today they are heading to his family's ten acres of rice fields. There on the 'crick dam' the forty to fifty feet of earthen berm that separated the well-known and usually fast flowing '66 creek' and the 'middle-walk' canal which supplied fresh black (tea-colored) water used to irrigate the crops, they planted a small but surprisingly productive vegetable garden.

His name was Jag. It was early in the morning. His mother to whom he referred to in his squeaky little voice as 'Mama', always wanted to start out early so that the neighborhood did not see a lady going to the fields and also to avoid the hot mid-morning sun on the long, tiring trek to the backdam. She wanted someone to accompany her to the fields and little Jag did not like that his mother would be going alone to the backdam. In his mind he was his Mama's protector.

They had already walked three quarters of a mile and past the ten feet wide by forty feet long wooden bridge called the 'drag-line bridge' which curved slightly upwards. The wooden structure straddled what was called the 'dragline' trench flowing north-south and helping to drain the rice fields. Today the brown, silt-laden water flowed swiftly, carrying with it green islands of floating grass left by the group of men who were clearing the drainage canals further inland. The water grasses threatened to cover the surface of all the canals and as soon as the men armed with their machetes hacked away and cleared a portion of the canal, within a few weeks it grew right back. (picture)

From this bridge the view opened up onto the wide expanse of green rice fields, stopped half a mile to the left by a thick forest of trees lining the '66 Creek' which snaked it's way four miles inland. To the right the open fields stretched as far as the eye could see. The bridge (picture) was covered with thick dried mud left by the farm tractors and the hundreds of muddy hooves of animals which were herded westwards, towards the savannah a few days earlier.

Over the muddy bridge the trail or 'dam' as it was called, was bordered by wild flowers and bushes that grew on the edges of the two parallel 'side-line' canals. Among these were different colors of a Canna Lily look-alike which stood proudly tall, and pointing at the blue sky topped by colorful flowers and numerous black seed pods. The twenty feet wide dam and parallel drainage canals stretched tiring miles out into the distance, disappearing into a thin gray line.

Twenty feet from the bridge, a dozen of so black carrion crows on the ground gathered on and around a discolored, bloody pile of rotting flesh which at one time was the body of a brown horse that enjoyed galloping the extensive trails and pastures in the area. They were large, bold and threatening birds with gruesome naked heads which were covered by a hood of mottled red-gray skin from which their inscrutable black eyes seemed to pierce the object of their attention.

A dozen more of these vultures were in the air and they made slow, lazy circle, casting fearsome shadows on the ground while looking for a chance to dive in and snatch their share of the feast. The suffocating stench of death was strong in the air. This forced the two travelers to cover their noses with their collars against the overbearing, oppressing stink. Shivering with dread, young Jag had to muster all his courage in order to pass by these big, ugly, ungainly-looking, big-beaked birds As mother and son walked quickly by, the creatures boldly kept on eating yet managed to keep a wary eye on the passersby. They seem ready to defend their feast with their ravenous, dirty beaks and needle-sharp talons if anyone dared to intrude. For about a quarter mile after passing these threatening birds, Jag kept looking over his shoulder until he felt that they were safely away from the fearsome creatures.

The tropical sun was up for only a half hour, but it was mid-July which was the beginning of the hot season and the heat was generating its playful, shimmering waves ahead on the brown-gray parched 'dam' leading to the rice fields. The tiny droplets of glistening dew leftover from the cool night slowly dissipated from the grass. The leaves of the bushes which lined the edge of the trail had refused the excess of the night dew and the dark, damp dots along the line where the bushes overhung the trail marked where these droplets have been swallowed by the dry earth. Mama encouraged her little son to take deep breaths of the leftover, feel-good, sweet fragrance of the secretive night wildflowers wafting in the gentle morning breeze. After the smell of death only a few minutes ago, this scent was a welcome and enticing mix of fragrance which created an almost mind-clearing experience. This made the long trudge in the wee hours of the morning seem almost worthwhile.

The trail (picture) was sliced by parallel deep drains made by the big farm tractors with their steel cage wheel-like contraptions attached to both huge back tires. These cage-wheels, (picture) as they were called, made the farm tractors almost unstoppable even when half of the large wheels were immersed in the thick mud which developed in the constant rains in the hot tropical climate.

His mud caked straw hat was perched upon his head at an angle and the wide brim hovered above his squinting eyes. His shoulder length hair seemed to sprout in jet-black unruly curls from beneath the dirty hat. With his eighteen inch machete gripped tightly in his right hand, he skipped bravely in and out of the clear, calm puddles of rainwater collected in the tire tracks. These pockets of water seemed massive compared to his diminutive size and his spindly legs, yet they measured no bigger than three to four feet wide, ten to thirty feet long and at most, three feet deep. (picture)

But in these seemingly innocent little ponds of water his mother saw danger. She kept looking back at him nervously, fully understanding the relief her little child must find from the hot clay in these cool puddles of water. But she worried about the invisible dangers of the rare broken glass bottles and thorns which may lurk beneath the calm surface of the water, or the lizards and snakes in the bushes, vines, thick 'Para grass' and wildflowers on both sides of the trail.

An hour after they left home, with Jag lagging behind, Mama stopped him for a short breather and a drink of water under the 'pasty tree' which marked about a third of their journey. This large tree with broad leaves bore bunches of greenish yellow fruits that the children used as glue on their paper kites and toys. It was also sweet, sticky, and messy to eat. Still, the little boy enjoyed a bunch with his mother constantly admonishing him "not to eat too much or you'll get sick".

Just ahead was the area known as the 'basin' named after the ancient utensils which were found in the area. Here Papa also owned an acre of rice land which never really did well. It seemed to always be on the verge of being over run by the spongy hollow-leafed 'busy-busy' grass, which left very little area for rice. The few hundred pounds of rice which was reaped from this land was done by hand using a sickle known locally as a 'grass-knife' The mature rice plants with the bunches of golden grains were cut about six inches off the ground then tied in huge bunches and loaded onto the back seat of the little Morris Minor to be transported home. At home the straw-like plants with attached golden grains were beaten against the ground, a standing post, or with a garden fork or the like, and the separated grains are then collected to be dried and processed.

Another a half hour of brisk walking, they stopped again at the bushy area known by all as the 'farm' for a drink of water and five minutes of rest. This was a quarter mile of almost wild, thickly forested area with mixed bushes, fruit trees and countless coconuts trees, almost all covered in some variety of green vines. In some small pockets a few trees could be seen being slowly smothered by an orange parasitic vine closely resembling spaghetti known as Dodder. This vine suffocated some of the large trees whose skeletons now stood bare, pointing lifeless fingers to the sky in the center of this otherwise lush area.

The large troop of spider monkeys that inhabited this isolated stand of wilderness scolded the passersby apparently for disturbing their peace, in their loud, funny chatter while swinging through the branches in slow graceful leaps. They numbered in the dozens and Jag was fascinated by these creatures that so skillfully and daringly seemed to defy gravity as they swung high up among the trees and vines. The group chattered incessantly until the two had walked way past before they quieted down. Mama was careful to make sure that Jag drank enough and as the blazing sun rose higher and the heat of the day grew she looked at him for signs of tiredness, since she knew that he was too proud to complain.

An hour and a half after they had left home through the almost-invisible gate in their back yard fence, they reached their first five acres of rice field. Here they had to cross over the 'side-line' trench. This canal had huge overgrown, tall floating islands of water grasses on the surface and tall para-grass overhanging on both banks into the water. This sight always scared him, for in his over-active ten-year old imagination, all the mean and scary creatures of the water lived there. To erase his fears in crossing this 'trench' his mother encouraged him to 'slap' the brown, silt-laden water with the broad side of his machete and assured him that the loud noise will scare away the snakes and alligators from their immediate crossing area. Slapping the water with the machete had its own risks however, since at even a small angle off, the blade seemed to slice uncontrollable through the water. Mama was careful to show him how exactly to hold the machete when doing this.

After slapping the water numerous times and listening in wonder at the loud, resonant 'whack' which echoed across the water, he grasp tightly onto his mother's right hand with his left and while brandishing his machete in the other, they quickly forded the waist-deep (to his mother) 'side-line' trench, the muddy water reaching almost to the little boy's neck, their feet slurping loudly in the knee-deep silt-mud on both banks.

After showing Jag how to regulate the water level by the 'cut' (an earthen berm across the ditch which drains the field, which when adjusted kept the water level in the flooded rice field at the desired level), they both walked through the eight inch high rice plants with Mama showing the little boy how to inspect the plants for the disease know as heart-worm, which ate the tender middle 'heart' of the little plants.

The next hour was spent tediously transplanting rice plants from areas where the plants were growing very thickly to the areas that were bare or had very few plants. Mama showed Jag how to uproot the 'beeya' as the transplanted rice plants were called and planting them one at a time in the bare spots. This was done by holding the single plant with its root laying and supported by the thumb sticking straight out, then plunging the thumb with the plant into the mud beneath the water and finally twirling the other fingers around to cover the root with the soft mud. Jag hated doing this chore, for there were all kind of scary bugs and leeches in the soft mud that usually clung to their bare feet and had to be scraped off with the machete.

He silently thanked God when Mama called it a day planting 'beeya'. The two then walked all the way to the back of the 'paddy' field, to the five feet high, ten feet wide 'middle-walk' dam where they had planted the popular root crop called cassava. They carefully uncovered a root area and checked the maturity of the cassava. Mama decided that they needed a few more weeks to get bigger before reaping to sell to the wholesalers at the Skeldon Market.

To the east, a huge black shadow cast on the green expanse of rice fields by a moving mass of dark gray-black clouds approached at great speed, blocking the hot rays of the sun. Within a few minutes, rain started as a fine spritz, which quickly became a thunderous downpour with the huge drops landing uncomfortably hard on the skin. Quickly, mother and son shook out two large sheets of plastic about four feet square which they had cut out from the lining of the empty fertilizer bags at home. These they used to covered themselves, crouching down between the cassava plants against the brisk wind-driven rain. In a few minutes, as quickly as it came, the rain stopped as the water logged clouds continued on their speedy journey west almost happily drenching everything along the way. The plastic sheets were then shook out, folded and tucked away for the next downpour.

The timid sun peeked out from the thin shining tail of the mass of clouds and in a few minutes, it blazed down triumphantly once again. Steam rose in white waves from the parched earth. The sweet almost intoxicating smell of hot earth and water permeated the air around them. Mama and Jag always enjoyed this pungent aroma after a quick rain shower and they did so now, breathing deeply for the next few minutes while it lasted.

Next, they crossed over the partially submerged bridge which was really only a slender tree trunk thrown between the banks of the 'middle-walk' canal which were about twelve feet apart, then walked through the tall 'busy-busy' grass that grew in the water-logged area to the bigger vegetable garden on the 'crick-dam'.

Here was the main farm and on the thick, loamy, rich, black soil, thick beds of healthy shallots, tomatoes, eggplant (bigan), pumpkin, squash, and mustard plants swayed in the now swift breeze. The tops of the Chinese radish roots poked whitely out of the black soil and its huge, edible, foot-long feather-like leaves whipped around lazily. Pumpkin vines wound triumphantly over and through the 'busy-busy' grass, it creepers supporting the big green leaves which sheltered the conquered green grass from the scalding sun. Every four or five feet, mid-sized pumpkins shone pale green against the deep green 'busy-busy' grass where they compressed the soft, spongy grass into the damp soil.

A few months ago, during the dry season when the 'middle-walk' canal water was quite low, a fire was set to burn off the encroaching grass. When a particular area refused to burn it was discovered that a humongous pumpkin about twenty inches high and about two feet in diameter had kept the surrounding grass damp so that it did not burn. Since this size of pumpkin was rare, it caused quite a stir when they took it home in the boat and a curious crowd gathered to watch two grown men struggle to carry the massive vegetable from the boat to the tractor. They could not get it to fit under the bed where Mama kept the pumpkins before selling them.

Next to the rushing black water of the 66 creek, the creepers of the round green squash, a cousin to the pumpkin, attempted to smother and subdue the bushes by snaking over and over itself. It's heavy globes of deep green vegetable hung high above the water supported by the bushes below. Retrieving some of these was a challenge as they hung on the far side over the deep water, almost beyond reach.

The neighboring farm to the east belonged to his father's brother Gowrinauth who everyone called 'Daad', and who he called 'Chacha'. (which meant uncle) His Chacha grew towering banana plants which made gentle rustling sounds as the broad leaves fenced against each other in the wind. To the west a medium sized sand-koker tree took advantage of the once open space and spread its canopy unimpeded across the entire 'dam'.

Jag helped to water the tomato, bigan (eggplant) and mustard plants using a small sheet metal bucket which they retrieved from its hiding place in the bushes. With Mama using a bigger bucket, they made numerous trips to the corner of the creek, went down a few muddy steps which were shoveled out in the riverbank. Here they dipped their buckets into the black water flowing in the creek which came out of the savannah a few miles to the west. A speedboat shot by heading east, surprising the two. The strong easterly winds kept the whine of the approaching outboard engine discreet, and suddenly it shot by sending its frothing wake crashing against the banks of the creek and for the next few minutes, smaller waves lapped over the feet of the two as they dipped their buckets into the water.

His mother gazed up at the sun that was almost directly overhead and decided that it was time for lunch. She retrieved the pot containing their lunch from the thing he called the 'island' which was a small heap of dirt surrounded by water which his mother made at the edge of the smaller canal. This was the only way in which they could keep the pot from being overrun by the black ants and other insects crawling all over the place. She then cut a large piece of a banana leaf about two feet square. Upon this leaf she placed lunch and together they ate rice, mustard and a dish made of fried tomatoes and onions which she knew her children loved.

After lunch, while his mother planted more mustard plants, Jag spent the next hour making a small boat out of a piece of the buoyant 'moko-moko' wood about twenty inches long and five inches in diameter, which he had snagged with a stick as it floated by in the swift running creek. With his machete, he hacked away at the soft, spongy, pulpy wood to shape a crude pointy boat. On the deep green, waxy side he scratched his name 'JAG' as big as he could. He waited until his mother was done with her planting and with her watching, and barely able to contain his exuberance, he proudly set his small green and white boat floating downriver, pushing it with a long stick into the middle of the creek. He jumped gleefully when it shot away in the swift moving current, right side up. They waited a few minutes until it was out of sight before returning to the task of picking vegetables to carry back on the long trek home.

Mama packed the little boy's bundle of vegetables in an empty and washed fertilizer (urea) bag which, when tied off and turned upside down, fitted and hung from his head like a cap, with the load of vegetables resting below his skinny little shoulders. Mama's bundle of vegetables was ten times the size of his, and this she balanced on her head all the way home. Except for a few which will be kept for home use, most of this load of vegetables which consisted of eggplant 'bigan', mustard greens, Chinese radishes, and a few oblong-shaped squashes, was to be sold to the wholesalers at the Skeldon market so Mama could balance the household budget.

Right before dusk they started their long trek back home. Along the way, Jag kept looking around in the bushes for the prettiest wild flowers which he picked and gathered in a small, fragrant and colorful bunch to give to his sister Shanie when they got home. He entertained himself by following in the tracks of a Land Rover, which dipped in and out of the mud. This vehicle had made its way to the fields sometime earlier in the day.

With the setting sun quickly dipping beneath the trees on the western horizon and the light slowly fading, the night flowers, welcoming the freedom of the coolness and approaching dark had started to release the almost intoxicating scent of their secretive night aroma which the two breathed in deeply as they tiredly walked on home.

As Mama walked she was focusing on a more practical wild crop, the finger-like flower of the moko-moko plant which she could use to prepare a meal for the family. Being one of the very few vegetarian families in Corentyne, they were the only ones who were known to cook the moko-moko flowers. When Mama spotted one she would put her load of vegetables down, go into the bushes, bend the spindly moko-moko plant over and snap off the flower.

Now the pot which had previously carried lunch, was almost full of the young moko-moko flowers (picture) which would do well towards a delicious meal the next day. Jag held tightly in his left hand, a bunch of fragrant wild flowers to present to his sister Shanie.

Halfway on the journey home, the gray mud-covered government Land Rover which had gone to the fields earlier came skidding and bouncing on its way back home, its engine whining and protesting at the incessant demands of the impatient driver. Mother and son stepped to the side of the trail to make way for the bouncing vehicle to pass by but instead it came to a skidding stop, mud slinging off the wheels in all directions. The driver, who was a distant cousin of Papa, poked his bearded face out of the dirty window and after greeting the two, asked whether they would like a ride for the remaining mile and a half of the journey. Mama, seeing her young son dragging his feet in exhaustion, gratefully accepted the ride home.

Rajkumaree Mahadeo 'Mama'

Rajkumaree Mahadeo was born on the 20th April 1932 to Sukhia and Sukhram, known to the rest of the family also as Ma and Pa. They had six children of whom Rajkumaree (Mama) was the eldest. Her siblings were Agamwatie, Mohanlall, Lookwanti, Roopnarine, and Bhoewatee.

Rajkumaree Mahadeo, known by all as 'Mama' was the emotional, magnetic force which held the family together through all the growing pains and occasional bickering of her five small children. She was the pivot point that supported the balancing act of her husband's busy public life with that of her family needs. Her husband was the well known political figure and Arya Samaj priest Pt. Budhram Mahadeo who was always in demand by the public because of his influential, shrewd, and tactful ways in helping people. He loved helping others so much that he was willing to risk the stability of his understanding family.

Mama's days were long and busy as she awoke early before sunrise to cook for her children before they left for school, after which she tended to the home vegetable garden in the backyard.

In the eyes of the neighboring villages, the family in the large house was rich and 'well-off', but that was far from the truth. Mama was the resourceful one who always found a way to, as she put it, 'make ends meet' or to make do with what she had. There were many days when, at that time unknown to her children, she went without a meal just so that everyone else in the family had enough to eat. Her husband, her two daughters, Vidya and Shanie and her three sons Vishwa, Jag and Yog were the focal point of her life and she made every effort to provide for them even if it meant sacrificing her own health. This totally unselfish behavior led to frequent bouts of migraine headache which she suffered through quietly.

Mama had no formal education but she was determined to learn more, so she spent any spare moment in her day with a book in hand trying to further her own education. She relied on this motivation to make sure that her children completed their homework and studied for their exams. She was determined to lead by example.

With this in mind, after a long, tiring day of weeding, forking the soil, raking, and planting, she sat diligently every night with her children to make sure that they did their homework. But as they learned, she did too. At the time, there was no electricity and all reading and homework was done by light of hand lanterns and kerosene 'gas' lamps which had to be pumped every ten minutes or so to keep burning. Along with academic studies she also taught herself to sing and to play the harmonium.

She is a caring, kind, and considerate person who knows not how to be harsh or mean. Mama exemplifies the perfect wife, mother, sister and daughter. Through her strength of character, she encouraged and influenced many of the decisions which her husband made in his life and was the towering strength behind his successes. She was also a great influence in the decisions her children made and would later make in their adult lives.

Mama took self development to new heights with her spiritual dedication and practice of meditation and communion with God. When people in the community approached her with their problems, she used her amazing ability in kindness, strength, love, perseverance, and her ever-calm demeanor to help them face the issues at hand. With this approach she helped them to resolve their problems in such a way that they would leave her home in a peaceful state of mind and a determination to take her advice to heart. She left with them the philosophical imprint of ultimate motherly love, for she saw everyone as her children.

Now, approaching her 80th year, she prefers to spend her days in peace and tranquility, lost in her practice of meditation and prayers, but with open arms for all those who may need her help or advice.

This is Rajkumaree Mahadeo, our mother, everyone's Mama (mother) and a symbol of integrity, strength, love, and caring. Her heart is one of total selflessness for she, like her husband, hold true to the belief that the purpose of their lives is service to all of Humanity.

Mid-Flight—Poem

When stuck at the eternal crossroads
And no sign of which way to go,
And any queries for help . . . . from without,
Seems answered with a profound 'NO'!

When Beauty and Purity is under siege,
. . . . broken promises, and hearts of stone reign,
And waves of chaotic heart-wrenching crying
When pure, tender, loving minds cannot stay sane.

When the flower garland that adorns the neck
Has been cruelly torn and ripped to shreds.
And it appears that the soul has deserted
And left the physical body for dead!

When the innocent, pure-white, love-angel
Has brushed lips with the devil's own,
And the place of red roses where doves flew
Now only thorns grow . . . . And deadly snakes roam.

If somehow crushed and left for dead,
Like the remains of rose petals underfoot.
The curtains of the eyes have been drawn shut
And life's whole purpose seems misunderstood.

When it feels like the devil's warped claws
Are painfully, deeply embedded in the flesh!
And the misfortunes befallen me is worthy,
For my past Karmas . . . . I haven't been blessed.

Let my perilous dark cloud that hovers overhead
Be pierced by one sword-blade of pure light,
Thus freeing my soul from the netherworld
In which I've been trapped in mid-flight.

Celebration of Holi (Phagwah)

Forty days before the Hindu festival of Holi, a site in the back of Number 64 Village was prepared for the building of the 'Holika' (bonfire). This was usually done by Louis Aja and a few other elders in the Mandir including Mahashay Aja, Birbal chacha and Silva chacha. The area which was selected for this symbolical ritual was an open grassy field where cows, horses, donkeys, sheep and all other animals grazed and frolicked. (picture)

Located a few hundred yards west was the village 'reef' farm with its vast expanse of towering coconut trees mixed in with mango, guava, and other cultivated fruit trees and wild native ones such as the ever-present 'jamoon'. This wide, grassy area was dotted with clumps of the 'carrion-crow' and black-sage bushes, many of which were being gradually smothered by the stranglehold of tenacious bushy vines.

In the next few weeks leading up to the fun festival, people piled twigs, leaves and dead branches from trees onto the spot, which gradually grew to quite a sizable heap. The youths of the No. 64-66 Village Arya Samaj Mandir led by Vishwa, would eventually make a few dedicated trips to the reef farms to gather discarded coconut palm fronds to add to this collection of combustible material and complete the building of the Holika. When completed this bonfire material stood about twenty feet high and about the same in diameter and jutted out of the surrounding flat area as if in pride, knowing that it will be the highlight of the celebrations to come, and the center of attention when it will cast its blessed light upon the entire village as far away as it can project itself in the total blackness of the Holi night. This night is also usually one of the darkest nights in the year.

Louis Aja made numerous trips daily to the site to keep a watch on the Holika. Some boys in the neighborhood were notoriously mischievous and Aja felt the need to make sure that no one messed with the precious bonfire. He also made his own frequent trips to add material to the pile.

In the weeks leading up to the festival, the 'chowtal' singing group comprising of the temple members, gathered at the home of different villagers who vied for their presence. At the villagers homes the singers and musicians awed the private audiences with their musical rendering which were mostly verses from the Hindu fable, the 'Ramayana'. This singing was a very loud event accompanied by drums, dhantals, and little brass cymbals which were held, one in each hand and clashed in time to the rhythm of the singing. After hours of energetic singing and celebrations they shared in the vegetarian refreshments prepared by the hosts before the evenings singing came to a close. This annual chowtal singing was a fun time for the youths in the area and they reveled in the joyous celebrations of Phagwah. The leaders of this group were Papa, Mahashay Aja, Louis Aja, Uncle Birbal and Uncle Silva. During these sessions Mahashay Aja kept busy fixing schedules for each night and make sure that everything goes as planned while coaching the youths in the singing of chowtal. These chowtal sessions were attended by many of the villagers and all in attendance reveled and laughed at the fun filled activities.

On the eve of Holi, which is observed on the full moon night in March, coconuts, ghee, honey, fresh fruits and vegetables etc, were added to the pile of flammable material. The light of day was slowly succumbing to the approaching, forceful blackness of the dark night. The entire Mandir congregation was in attendance and together with much of the neighborhood, they all gathered by the sacred bonfire. Special Havan (rituals) was performed to the chants of Vedic mantras and the Holika was set ablaze during the chants. At first the small flame cautiously licked at the religious offerings than discovered the tempting, dry branches beyond waiting to be devoured and seemed to pounce, quickly spreading, popping and crackling in glee as it enveloped the entire vertical, pyramid looking structure.

The bright yellow, almost smokeless flames feeding on the dry fuel shot into the night sky in triumph, trying to reach its flaming fingertips as high as it could to cast its grand light in a vain effort to finally defeat the dark enveloping blanket of night. In addition to a change in seasons, this grand spectacle symbolizes the victory of good deeds over evil forces and of devotion surpassing greed. Holi reminded everyone to burn all the impurities of the mind such as greed, lust, anger, egotism, jealousy and vanity, through the fire of devotion and knowledge and ignite love, kindness, selflessness and goodness in themselves and each other.

Dozens of ears of delicious corn were roasted in the holy fire and shared among all the revelers who seemed spellbound by the sight of the huge crackling inferno. Even when there were no corn planted in the area, Louis Aja made sure that he found some which he would roast in this 'sacred fire' and then share a few kernels to each of the attendees. On this auspicious occasion this was his way of sharing his kindness, love and caring.

On the next day known as Phagwah, some of the sacred ashes from the bonfire are collected and after a ceremony at the Mandir, smeared on the forehead and lightly all over the body by everyone. Then the entire congregation had fun dousing each other with water, colored water called 'abhir' and powders of many different colors. It was a fun festival especially for the children who reveled in the colorful all-day play with each other. The sight of hundreds of people whose once-white clothing were now red, green, blue, yellow and a mix of other colors seemed to make the heart lighter and problems somehow seemed non-existent on this auspicious day. Smiling, happy faces were smeared with white, red and blue powder and the white powder made many heads of jet black hair, gray-looking as everyone had a grand, enjoyable time.

The No. 64-66 Village Arya Samaj Mandir was an old, well maintained single storey structure about fifty feet deep and forty feet wide with a high steeple like tower about fifteen feet from the back in which a family of bats always found refuge. Because of the Hindu belief of non-violence and kindness to all living beings, the little colony of bats lived there undisturbed for many, many years. The building was about five feet above the ground with wide steps leading up to the entrance. In the rear, a small door led down narrow steps into the back yard where a small hut was used to house an old man who was the caretaker of the Mandir some years ago.

The rough, sandy area underneath the structure of the temple was pockmarked with wide shallow holes which were dug by dogs and the occasional pig that snuck into the fenced in yard. This cavernous area was used by many of the more adventurous children to play their games of hide and seek between the supporting concrete columns of the Mandir. This was also where Jag's dog Rio used to wait upon him until the Sunday sermon ended before walking home with him.

In the front yard flowering plants such as zinnias and marigolds were planted on flower beds along the front fence. Hedges of henna grew tall along both side fences. The flowers of this plant were used to make the paste for painting the distinctive Indian 'Henna' skin art. The flowers also exuded a tantalizing sweet aroma which caused one to catch ones breath in anticipation of the next whiff of the alluring scent riding on the gentle wind.

After the Mandir services and a lot of Phagwah playing, a flatbed truck was arranged to take everyone including the singing 'chowtal' group to visit the sick and less-fortunate members of the community. This was the elders' way of encouraging and including them in the festivities, talk and feed them some of the sacred sweets which were blessed in the Mandir early that morning. Prayers were also offered for their good health and well being

The arrival at the home of the sick was noisy with the loud singing of 'chowtal' which stopped at the door of the house. There, in a somber mood, everyone filed in and gathered at the bedside of the sick person and included them in the joyous playing of Phagwah. Pandit Budhram Mahadeo then led everyone in prayers for health and healing. Here Louis Aja perfected the compassionate role in his offering of the sweet used in the Mandir a few hours ago to the sick person.

This annual practice of tolerance, compassion, love and kindness to the less fortunate at a time of much celebration was added to the festivities of Holi by Pandit Raghubir and Pandit Mahadeo and has become an annual practice by the temple. These visits to the sick at this time of joy and reveling in this small community taught the entire congregation, especially the young children, the importance of sharing their love, compassion and joy and to feel empathy for others. It left a distinct and lifelong impression in the younger generation which guided and determined how most of them would later live their lives as adults.

Louis Aja

Louis Aja was man of small physical stature, but of formidable mental strength. This was displayed in his stubborn defense of his religious and philosophical beliefs. He had no formal schooling and except for his broken English, no one could tell that he never went to school. He gained his wisdom over the years from his own experience and those of others and he used everything he learned to fine-tune his charisma and charm as he aged. His sense of compassion was refined by his care and dedication to his sickly wife. This compassion was borne with an intense pride which lit up his face whenever he was observed caring for her.

This calm and humble old man known to everyone only as 'Louis Aja' was one of the gentle souls who were never heard to say an unkind word about another fellow being. Because of a back injury a long time ago, he walked bent over at the waist and as he aged, his stoop became more pronounced until in his later years he was totally bent over from the waist. Even with all of this, he was never once heard to complain about his misfortune or his pain.

His dedication to Pandit Budhram Mahadeo was well known and very evident by the reverence and devotion which he showed in Papa's presence. In his everyday life he showed this as he tried to put all his Pandit's teachings into practice.

He was a tailor by trade and sewed most of the 'Kurtas' and 'kurta pants' that the members of his Mandir wore. The youths would go to his home where he took their correct measurement and lovingly sewed their religious garments to precisely fit their growing frames. His calm, peaceful demeanor almost demanded that everyone responded in kind to him and he was much loved by everyone, especially the children. His voice was soft and gentle and complemented his kind and generous personality. His voice was never heard raised in displeasure or anger at anyone.

Because of his selflessness, he was the self appointed caretaker of the Mandir facilities and made sure that all materials, from the 'dhoop' wood used in the sacred fire to the ghee, spices, and flowers, were available in time for services on Sundays or for any special mid-week occasion. The brass utensils used in the rituals of the Mandir were washed and kept at his home which was always open to all. Even on days when the Mandir was not used, he came in to open the many windows at sunrise and closed them at dusk.

When the 'backdam' dams or trails which the tractors and people used to access the rice fields would be flooded out by rainfall, even though he did not use these trails, Aja would take his shovel and walk the four miles length of the trail, filling the holes by shoveling as much dirt much as his frail body would allow.

He was quiet, almost saintly in his demeanor and rarely spoke, but when he did, they were soft-spoken words of kindness, love and caring.

This was our Louis Aja. He embodied dedication and loyalty and used not words to tell how to be, but his actions to show how to be. He became the epitome of caring, kindness, and compassion.

"Son, think good thoughts and do good things and God will bring good to you."

Louis Aja

Mahashay Raghubir Aja

Mahashay (Teacher) Raghubir was a man of strict ethics and a behavioral code in which his every action was fore-thought and measured. He was the truest example of the man who stood tall for his beliefs and refused to take a single step backwards, refusing to compromise in any way, in his quest to excel in his personal life, and in helping others.

He was the spiritual teacher of Pandit Budhram Mahadeo and he came to be very proud of his exceptional student.

His quiet, contemplative, demeanor was one that made those in society of lesser morals uncomfortable in his presence even though he was not one to demean others under any circumstances. He was the teacher of all and was the most respected of the elders of the Number 64-66 Village Arya Samaj Mandir. Here every Sunday, he took the opportunity to impart his wisdom on the congregation in a way which was quite unique. At each Sunday's service he gave lectures on topics which were not only religious, but practical to every day life. An example of this was when one Sunday when he asked everyone to take home with them a question, think of the answer all week and come next Sunday with their best answer. The question was 'What is the key to happiness in one word?' The following Sunday every person came with their own answer or explanation and of course, they were all incorrect. He calmly gave the answer as 'Contentment' and through his unique and gentle way of speaking; he explained his answer using very simple language and analogies so that the children could receive and understand his full message.

He was the most vocal during the weeks leading up to the celebrations of the immensely popular Phagwah (Holi) festival which was sometime in March. (depending on the Moon's position in the sky) This was when his loud resonant voice would be above everyone else in the daily group singing of 'Chowtal' in each other's homes. Here he led the youths in learning the words and vocalizing them in his unique way. This interaction with the youths made the singing of 'chowtal' a yearly treat for the young minds in his care.

His countenance was always of one deep in thought and one felt a sense of awe and utmost respect in his presence. He was never without one of his many philosophical books from his home library, which made up a good portion of his bedroom, or a pen and paper upon which he scribbled his thoughts. In his home were furniture which he built with his own hands and a black board on which he wrote while trying to impart his wisdom to his grandchildren or occasional visitors. He was always willing to teach and spent many years teaching Hindi at the Tagore Memorial High School.

At a time when most people were hesitant to have their daughters out of the house, he broke the mold and sent his daughter to the Guyana Teacher's Training College far away in the country's capital of Georgetown. This very act sent a message of liberation to other young women and made them feel empowered and free in actually seeking a career and independence from the expectation of just being a housewife who helped in the fields.

He was the family counselor for many families and together with Louis Aja, Pandit Mahadeo, Uncle Birbal, Uncle Silva, and a few others they formed the 'Panchayat' which in Indian tradition was the assembly of five wise and respected elders chosen and accepted by the community. This group helped to resolve many of the community issues at the time.

His days in his later life were spent researching and trying to further his education and spirituality. His leadership style was one of leading by example and this he did with great vigor. He was a great soul who encouraged everyone, especially the children to reach for the stars.

He was a great motivator and coach and there are many today who owe their way of life and value system to him and his teachings.

This was our much beloved Mahashay Aja, a staunch believer in people, God, spirituality, and the need to continuously improve the Self in this classroom of life.

"Question: What is the key to happiness in one word?
Answer: Contentment!"

Pandit Mahashay Raghubir

Little Boy Knee deep in mud—Poem

Bare-footed Little Boy, knee-deep . . . . in mud he dread
Dirty straw hat perched jauntily a-top his head.
Following his loving mother's every move
And skipping in and out of tractor-tire-made grooves

On sun-baked spots of earth, his naked-bottomed feet burns
while nimbly jumping over sticks and prickly thorns.
Little Boy walked four long miles to the farm,
in mind, to protect his dear Mother from harm.

Scared of creatures crawling on the ground
Mean birds, bees, and wasps flying around.
Leeches in the stinking mud, crawling up his bare legs
Sucking blood and looking like small, long black eggs.

Little Boy and Mother in wind-blown rain,
Walking covered in clear plastic . . . . but in vain.
They are both dripping wet and soaked to the skin,
But they dried up hours later when the sun win.

Now in the blazing sun, keeping his mother company,
Tired, squinting eyes can barely see.
Little Boy helped with whatever he could
or was busy making boats out of moko-moko wood.

Little Boy in old, dirty, mud-caked clothes,
Soft dark-gray mud squishing up between his toes
Bruises and scrapes from falls . . . . and bumps from insect stings.
Tossing stones in the water . . . . making ripple-rings.

Right before sunset, home they went.

Totally exhausted . . . . all their energy spent.
Little Boy scrubbed, showered and now clean,
Sleeping in his straw filled bed, the little boy dream,

Of the farm and the bugs, and the flowers and buds,
And of the Little Boy trudging knee-deep in mud

*   *   *

The Reef Farm

For a few years, one of the Mahadeo's vegetable farms was across from the sand-reef drainage canal and almost a quarter mile farther west in an area known by everyone as the 'Reef'. Here Mama planted tomatoes, 'bigan' (eggplant), 'bora' (asparagus beans) black-eyed peas and urad peas in the rich reddish-brown sandy soil. After keeping enough of the crops for household use, Mama usually sold the rest of the produce to wholesalers to supplement the household income. Today, the whole family accompanied Mama to help at the farm. Watering all the plants was quite a time consuming chore and all the Mahadeo children pitched in, using old paint cans and buckets to carry water from the drainage canal fifty to one hundred feet away.

To get to the reef farm meant walking through Number 65 Village and along a narrow path through the jungle-like mango trees and bushes or going around over the drag-line bridge and across the walk-bridge to the farm. At the farm surrounding the thirty-six feet by one hundred and fifty feet planting area, there were stands of 'awara' palm, the plum sized fruits which, when ripe, had about a one-eight inch thick orange skin that was fibrous and chewy but also succulent and tasty. These tall palms trees that grew in the wild had to be approached very carefully since every part of it, from the trunk to the fronds, was protected by a thick coat of one to two inch long, needle-sharp thorns.

There were also numerous 'jamoon' trees which bore a sweet, purple, grape-sized fruit with a quarter inch hard seed in its center. Any open area between these tall trees was thickly forested with the pungent black-sage bushes, 'bitas' and castor oil plants. Beyond these bushes were coconut trees stretching for many miles north. These tall, spindly-looking trees, topped with multiple fronds and bunches of coconuts, danced and swayed in rhythm to the lightest breeze. On a windy day dried coconuts could be heard falling, crashing through the dense, vine-choked undergrowth and thudding into the sandy soil below. These were later collected by the farmers to make coconut oil which was used by everyone for cooking, for its medicinal properties and massaging of tired bodies after long, hard days of work in the rice fields. A vine which grew claws that resembled a bird's feet, used these ingenious creations to claw its way up the trunks of these trees and grew thickly as it intertwined upon itself.

At the time the wildlife inhabiting these bushes were surprising in number and variety. Dozens of different types of colorful and melodious birds, butterflies, wild dogs called 'crab-dogs' because of their diet of wild crabs and every type of stinging insect imaginable to the little boy lived in these bushes. Red ants (fire ants) was prevalent and always a threat. This aggressive ant made their nests in the ground in the most unexpected places, and if a nest was stepped on, in seconds they would be crawling up the legs by the dozens and stinging in every spot imaginable. The stings left red marks and were very painful. Frightful looking, large reddish-brown locusts covered the 'bitas' plants and climbed over each other making loud buzzing sounds when disturbed.

These frequent trips to the farm were fun and adventurous and today, with their father's protection, all the children felt free to roam around looking for wild fruits and berries.

The beds of tomato which the family planted stretched for about fifty feet by about twenty feet wide and the healthy, deep green foliage seemed to be lit up by countless bright red tomatoes ready to be picked. The sweet pungent scent emanating from the tomato plants hung temptingly in the still air. After watering all the plants and many hours of hoeing and pulling weeds, the family joined together to gently harvest ripe tomatoes by hand and placed them carefully into baskets and buckets so they stayed in perfect shape for selling after the trek home. A few of the 'bigan' were also ready to be picked and these were carefully packed to avoid bruising, which would also lower the price. A small water melon and a ripe yellow and fragrant 'musk-melon' were plucked from their vines to the delight of the children, who looked forward to this special treat at home.

Jag was tasked with pulling up the dried 'urad' plants with bunches of dried pea pods and stuffing the entire plants into a big urea bag. Mama would later 'beat' these dried plants with a flat piece of board called a 'pitna' which was normally used to wash clothes. This process of beating released the peas from the pods. They are then collected for cooking the 'urad' dhal—a pea soup like gravy which is eaten with rice and roti.

At dusk, with the sunlight slowly fading, the family made their way back home with the baskets of tomatoes and eggplants balanced on their heads and Jag carrying the comparatively light but big bag of dried pea plants on his head.

Fountain of life—Poem

Drink deep from the Fountain of Life,
And highly value every precious drop.
You never know when this running stream,
will come to a sudden and complete stop!

Enjoy every experience and tender moment,
Let not a day or a minute, go to waste,
Much to do and so much to enjoy,
So you'd better get up . . . . And make haste.

Carefully plan, know exactly what you want.
And please establish yourself a goal.
Cause father time waits for no one and
Before you know it, you will be old.

Stop and take a careful step back
Every so often, once in awhile,
Reflect and look at yourself
Through someone else's eyes.

Be cautious and listen to your voice
Make it pleasant to your own ear.
Cause in that same tone of voice,
All the responses you will hear.

Let your God, your own intuition,
Be your dear and closest ally,
After all, it is your constant guide
And rarely . . . . almost never lie.

And try to never give your opinion,

Unless it is wanted and requested
You won't make friends this way,
Not many like a know-it-all or like to be bested.

Try your utmost to never ever lie
Especially not to those who you love,
The time it takes to mend a broken heart,
Sometimes this fountain does not have enough.

And show all of your fellow souls
The same high degree of respect,
That in your daily dealings with them
You . . . . will come to expect.

Learn from the mistakes of others,
And from those that you will certainly make
Or life will be like the chaotic ocean,
Instead of the peace and calmness of a small lake

Stand proud; keep your shoulders straight,
And hold your head proud and up high.
Show pride in your every step,
And life will prove out the reasons why.

Remember, life just keeps going,
And time is not, your friend.
The fountain of life is flowing,
But soon it will come to an end.

So drink deep of this precious fountain,
And try to make your happiness.
Measure all your successes wisely,
And always try to act your best.

Learning to be a Pandit

Pandit Budhram Mahadeo was smartly dressed in his white Kurta and his elaborate, well-fitting Dhoti and his second son Jag was proudly dressed in his white pants and Kurta. Around nine in the morning, they left in his Papa's car to perform a Havan ceremony for Lawyer Pawaroo and his family in an area known as Bengal. While driving, his father nodded or raised his hand occasionally in acknowledgement to the raised hands of people walking along the road or passing by in cars going in the opposite direction. Pandit was a well known and highly respected person and he always acknowledged people wherever he went. During the half hour drive, he took the opportunity to help his second son learn some of the Vedic mantras, with which he was having some difficulty, by slowly guiding him in the proper recitation of the mantras. His loud, resonant, yet peaceful voice echoed in the confines of the small car as he chanted and he had his son slowly repeat the chants after him.

Like his other two brothers Vishwa and Yoganand, and sisters Vidya and Shanie, Jag was also a Pandit in training as his father wished them all to be. They always spent moments like these reciting the Sandhya, Havan or other Vedic mantras or practicing singing some of Papa's favorite religious bhajans. Papa saw this not only as a way to get his children on what he was convinced to be the righteous path, but to hopefully mold their sense of values and cultivate them into a lifelong force of helping others. He made a personal habit of coaching his children to make speeches, sing bhajans (religious hymns) and interact in the very public forum of the Havans he conducted.

He encouraged and stimulated their philosophical thinking by organizing frequent, sometimes-spontaneous debate sessions among his children on topics such as 'life after death', 'the presence of God' and his personal favorite 'service to mankind'. During these debates his children, especially Vishwa and Shanie, would sometimes become so animated and loud that Papa would have to forcefully interject himself in the role of the peacekeeping facilitator. He loved that his children took these sessions so seriously and they in turn, loved the fact that he showed his pride in them and their active participation. These animated and fun discussions instilled into his children the courage to stand by their values and never to compromise them. All the five young Mahadeo children grew up to be strong, confident and very secure in presenting themselves in public forums.

Upon arriving at the host family's home, Jag held his head up proudly as he walked beside his father to take his place next to him by the Havan 'kunda'. Here he sat stiffly upright in the lotus posture as his father led the congregation of about two hundred people in the chanting of Vedic mantras in the Havan ceremony. When the sacrificial fire was lit, (picture) the little boy was responsible for keeping the ceremonial fire going while he chanted and tried to match his father's deep voice in pride. He was very conscious of his squeaky 'little-boy' voice and could not wait to get his Papa's voice—like his Mama told him he would when he grew up.

The Havan sermon, chanting, singing and other contributions from guests, took about two and a half hours. When the ceremony was completed, the 'prasad' (sweetmeats after the religious service) was served, and then the entire congregation sat in neat rows on the floor. After reciting a mealtime prayer led by Pandit Mahadeo, they enjoyed the elaborate vegetarian meal prepared by the hosts for this annual occasion. The meal of puri, aaloo curry, kheer, dhal, rice and many other delicacies, was served on the big green leaves of the lotus plant which were cut and stocked just for this occasion. As was the practice, the meal was eaten with the fingers.

To help guide his children, give them practice, instill confidence, and improved their knowledge of conducting the Havan ceremony, Papa occasionally arranged for each of his children to conduct ceremonies for the public by themselves, usually starting with the thirteen successive nights of Havan which some families chose to perform after the death of a family member.

He used patience and coached each of them to become proficient public speakers by encouraging them to make short speeches at these occasions and even at home when they did their family birthday Havans. The Mahadeo children celebrated each of their birthdays with a birthday Havan. In these ceremonies, they used a garland of flowers and loose flower petals to convey their best wishes and blessings upon the one celebrating his or her birthday. They have continued this tradition in later years with their own children.

The leadership skills which Papa showed in public was tactfully used to mentor, motivate and teach his own children his values and how to respectfully conduct themselves as fellow Pandits. This he did best the way all great leaders do, by setting the example for them to follow.

These leadership skills which were instilled in his children by Pandit Budhram Mahadeo was continually enhanced over the years and would later heavily influence the path that each of them chose as a career.

"From the first day on earth to the last, we are on a quest for knowledge. Never stop learning, for it is the only path to enlightenment"

Pandit Budhram Mahadeo (Papa)

Body To Mind—Poem

There are countless times in our lives when even though our bodies may be healthy; our minds are in an extreme state of confusion. At these times, it seems like we cannot control our minds. It is hard to concentrate properly and our poor bodies are at the mercy of the uncontrollable mind.

The following is written as if the body is talking to the mind about this confused state, just as a servant talking to a master. It is titled **Body to Mind.**

My dear Mind, why do you fail me like this?
Why do you let Emotions rule you?
Why do you not listen to your conscience?
And keep only what is good to keep?

My Mind, why do you choose to do the things,
Which are harmful to me, your body?
Why do neglect me in times of dire need?
Why do you entertain unhealthy thoughts,
that does nothing but cause misery for you
and tremendous pain for me, your body?

My Mind, you wander about sometimes?
Like a little child, picking up
so many little things of no use to you or me?
You keep them all tucked away inside
to add to the confusion in you
when we already face so much turmoil around us.

My Mind, why do you often entangle yourself
in that web of deceit, lies, corruption
and impulsive behavior?

I expect you, my Mind,
to control those impulsive thoughts
but you do not help me.

Without controlling these impulses,
you have made me, your body fall prey to addictions,
which cause me immense pain and
make me deteriorate faster than my age.

My Mind, you have not yet distinguished
between hunger and appetite.
You make me satisfy the craving for drugs,
alcohol and foods that are bad for me
which instead of nourishing me, punishes me.
My Mind, you do not guide me, Instead,
to satisfy simple hunger with healthy foods,
you make me "live to eat instead of eating to live".

Do you not think of me Mind?
My health relies so much on you
but you choose to ignore me.
You choose not to give me sound sleep and rest.
My Mind, you insist on interrupting my rest
with your constant juggling of useless thoughts
and terrible fantasies.
Your ceaseless wandering make me gnash my teeth
and toss and turn in my sleep.
I am physical, Mind. I need rest.

My Mind, you think on and on of other people,
most of whom will not help in making us happy.
Are you not the one who should be in control, Mind?

I wait for permission from you,
from you my Mind,
before attempting to do any action.
You are the one I wait on to make decisions for me.
I do nothing without you.

I AM nothing but an empty shell
Without you, My Mind
But you disappoint me so!
Why?

My Mind, so many times you have instructed me
to do things which after doing,
left me filled with nothing but pain.
So many times you have instructed me to do things
that have hurt our loved ones.
Why do you give yourself permission
to entertain bad and unreasonable thoughts
and make me, your body, suffer like this?

You make yourself like an open room, Mind.
You leave all your doors
and all your windows open and let
any strange thoughts wander in,
then you welcome them,
hold them close
and make them your guests.

When you do this My Mind, you can never sit in a moment of silence
to contemplate the things that would make you
and in turn, me better.
When you try to concentrate,
all your guests get in your way.
You are never alone.
You can never enjoy solitude
with the atmosphere
you have created in your room, Mind.

My Mind, you choose not to protect
that which you are supposed to hold sacred.
You let others change you
in whatever way they want.
They mold you like play putty.
You take in whatever garbage

that others give you, Mind.
You harbor gossip and idle talk.
You meddle in the affairs of others
without solving your own problems first.

You have not lived up
to your true potential, Mind,
but yet, you try your best to impress others
with the little that you know.
At times you have made me act
because of Ego, Mind.
You keep polishing this Ego, this false pride.

Mind, Sometimes you have made Ego
look like the master and
we all have had to suffer the indignation,
the hurt and the scars
with which Ego leaves us.
You should know better
than to let Ego override our simple pride.

Now, consider me.
Think of me, Mind.
I may only be your Body,
but I am the medium
that makes you visible to the world.
I am the one that acts on your behalf
and the one that make the sounds that form speech.
All of these with your permission of course!
The speech from my lips is composed
of the thoughts that you, my Mind, send forth.

Therefore, others will judge you
Through me, your body!
They will judge me by my actions,
the pride with which I carry myself,
and the EGO messages you send.
They will judge by the words that I choose

and the tone of voice that I use,
and through my words and actions,
you, ... my Mind . . . . will be judged.
Think of **_THAT_** My Dear Mind.

Baby Rats

It was three in the afternoon when Jag came home from school on his bicycle, his 'Big-Ben' bike, which years ago had belonged to his father when he was a young man. Tagore Memorial High School was about a mile away and most children in the area either walked or rode their bicycles to school. His bike had no brakes and as most of the kids did, he had perfected the practice of using his bare feet or his sandals against the smooth and shiny back rim to stop the bike. He wheeled his bike over the bridge into the yard, noting that the bushes around the bridge once again needed cutting back. The thick, green vegetation and water grasses surrounding the ditch in front of the house, grew fast and required cutting back every few weeks. Jag or his brothers usually helped doing this, using a machete and slashing at the vines and weeds to keep the area around the bridge and in front of the house clear.

After changing from his school uniform into his 'house clothes', and an early dinner of rice and fried eggplant and dhal, he undertook the occasional task of selling some vegetables from their garden to the villagers. Mama had already packaged the 'parcels' of produce in a shallow woven basket which he balanced on top of the bicycle handlebars and kept in place with one hand. The basket contained a few breadfruits, parcels of eggplant, bora (asparagus beans) and okra. Slowly he rode through all the streets of the three villages while calling out to each home "Do you want to buy breadfruit, 'bigan' and bora?" With a favorable answer he would wait until the housewife inspected the vegetables, make their selection and pay the proper amount in cash. When he had completed the rounds of all three villages, he headed home to give his Mama the good news of the entire sale he had for the afternoon.

He then grabbed his red 'Craven A' bag of books and clambered up onto the bags of unshelled rice, 'paddy' stacked in one corner of the 'bottom-house' against the concrete wall. The big bags were stacked about eight to ten bags high. At the top he had created a cubbyhole by moving around a few of the one hundred and twenty pound bags of rice. This he had struggled with on his own for a few days. The rough texture of the rice bags had bruised his knees in his effort to create his little fort. Here he would lie down and after many days of use, the forgiving bags had molded around his body somewhat, to become a comfortable reclining seat, with his skinny legs propped up on another bag of rice.

From this vantage point he could see the area where he and his elder brother Vishwa got in trouble with Mama a few months ago. They were shooting green goose-berries (picture) at a target with their father's spring operated pellet gun and used the laundry hanging on the line to dry as the backdrop for their target. These berries fitted perfectly into the chamber of the pellet gun. The countless exploding berries which missed their target left splotches of green on the sheets and the other clothes on the line. Mama was at first confounded by the stains until one day she finally caught the two of them shooting the berries at the coconut tree in the back yard.

When Buddy got the pellet gun from Papa he also had enough lead pellets with it to use for a few days. Then the pellets ran out. After days of looking around and experimenting with different things to substitute as pellets, Buddy discovered that the bunch of goose-berries which he brought home from his trip to the rice fields worked really well. Cranking the pellet gun was hard and Jag relied on his brother to help him until he developed the strength to do it himself. His elder brother was patient in doing this and showing him how to hold and aim the gun. A few times they sneaked out to go shooting by the creek and took turns shooting at selected targets across the creek and the items floating by in the fast moving water. He remembered the many times when he and his elder brother took aim at the crabs crawling by the side of the creek but they could not bring themselves to take a shot at a living animal.

Now comfortable in his hideout atop the paddy bags, he spent the next hour reading his comic books. The strong, pleasantly dusty smell of the sun-dried paddy contained in the bags upon which he sat, enveloped him within his fort and he enjoyed it. He could hear his brother 'Buddy' talking and strategizing to his group of guys who made up his cricket team about the game that he was planning against the team from the neighboring village. After a while he dozed off with his open book flat upon his chest.

He was awakened from his short slumber by some high pitched squeaking noises coming from under him and it spurred his memories to a few days ago. From this vantage point, he had followed some squeaking noises that beckoned to him and he had found a rat's nest with a half dozen baby rats squirming about in a mix of dried grass and golden-yellow, paddy grains. (Un-shelled rice) The rats had chewed open a bag of paddy and here they had made a warm and comfortable home for their babies. He had picked up the tiny pink creatures and played with them. Their inside organs of varying hues of red and dark showed through their transparent skin. Their eyes were as yet unopened, and were just dark blobs showing through the tiny pink eyelids. Their feet were tiny, rubbery and useless. He had played with them and decided to name them after the seven dwarfs from the book Snow White, which he had read a while ago. But there was a problem since there were seven names and only six rat babies. This, he solved by also naming the missing mother. He named the babies as Sneezy, Sleepy, Dopey, Doc, Bashful, Grumpy, and named the missing mother who he never saw, 'Happy' since he thought that she would be happy to have the six pretty little babies. Problems persisted however, since he had a hard time identifying them. They all looked and behaved alike except for Bashful who always tried to find a corner to stick his head into. Even when he was picked up by Jag, Bashful would stick his head into the crease between his thumb and palm.

Sitting is this cubbyhole among the rice bags, young Jag was warm and comfortable. Here he spent many afternoons doing his homework and extra school work. Sometimes he stayed long after he was done and would eventually doze off until he was called by his mother to shower or for a late dinner.

"Every one of God's creation, every life, weather it is a plant or an animal is our brothers and sisters. We are like the elder brother and sister who should protect and take care of all of them, not destroy them for our gains"

Rajkumaree Mahadeo (Mama)

My purpose . . . . PLEASE?—Poem

We are born "a bundle of joy",
To our siblings, a baby toy.
To some, a "bundle of pain",
Born sick, helpless and nothing to gain.
Why am I here?

"Growing up" we are told, is . . . . supposed to be fun,
But for many millions of kids, they have none.
Growing up to about ten years of age,
The book of life then turns another page.
Why is this?

From here on, try to meet all the standards set,
So many of these, will never be met.
Try to walk the straight line between good and bad,
For so many kids, it's always so sad.
What is the reason?

At fifteen years of age, so confused, so unsure.
These questions keep coming up more and more.
Girls and drugs, liquor and abuse,
Sometimes I feel so confused, of no use.
Do I really even exist?

Struggle all the way through school,
Tried to make education a useful tool.
I am so very gullible at this age,
I found part-time work for below minimum wage.
Is this worth it?

Just like a bucket full of crabs,
Seem like everyone wants to grab.
To drag me down, it's such a fight,
To keep doing what I think is right.
Is this fair?

Out of college now . . . . there four years,
Tried to have some fun while I was there.
I really tried very hard, I did my best,
Got mostly A's in most of my tests.
Will this really help?

The struggle continues, buried in debt.
On not finding a good job, I never did bet.
Temptations draw me over the edge,
I cling desperately with, fingertips at the ledge.
Why do I live?

Finally settled down, became a family man,
All the ups and downs, I mostly won.
But just when I thought I figured life out,
My good health just started going south.
Is this life?

In my forty's, very well I can't see.
Why is my health going downhill on me?
Cannot do the things I used to do,
Can't even hear your words ring true.
Is this it?

At fifty, I decide to face the fact,
Getting older kinda knocks you on your back.
It's something that all of us have feared.
Now I put up with mental and bodily wear.
Where does this life lead to?

I cannot bend down, I cannot sleep,

Pain in me makes me want to weep.
I am so tired day to day,
I feel like I have lost my way.
Is life really worth it?

At sixty, I have arthritis in my bones,
I can no longer even touch my toes.
All my aching joints, they feel so tight,
I cannot understand my terrible plight.
Why is this happening to me?

At seventy, I am going blind,
I can't even think with a straight mind.
My body aches, my hands shake,
Don't know how much of this I can take.
Where am I going from here?

No Priest from any religion,
Ever really answered my questions
They all have given it a whack,
But it is a tough one to crack.
Do the answers even exist?

So many theories but no one could prove,
Why are we here? Why do we move?
Or are we a figment of the imagination,
Of some higher, more powerful creation.
Why am I here?

Of death I have now started to think,
I feel I am very close to the brink.
I often wonder, has it all been in vain?
What have I accomplished? What have I gained?
Or is this all a dream?

Finally, now that I am dead,
My body placed on its eternal bed.
All of my life, questions endless,

No real answers, Oh what a mess?
All of the struggle, all the strife,
What exactly was the purpose of my life?

The Village Master's Roost

The huge tamarind tree grew ten feet away from the pale, pink-red edge of the veranda railings and the thick, dark, rough trunk which skinned many shins and hands of its climbers over the years, snaked past the gutter and overhang of the roof only five feet away. Here Papa made sure that he trimmed the branches away to prevent access to the roof from the tree. However, Jag being as agile as a monkey, did not find it difficult to stand at the edge of the roof, fling himself out and grabbing onto the smaller, yet flexible and strong limbs. This he did many times when he teased his sister or his Nanee. (Mother's Mom) He was very mischievous and after teasing them he would scamper up his tree. While they waited for him thinking that he was still in the tree, he would make his way down over the roof and do what he needed to do in his room. Above the roof, the tree branched off and towered past the third floor tower and prayer room. Here it spread its deep green branches to the sun in a canopy about forty feet in diameter, threatening to engulf and overpower the red painted metal roof of the neighbor's house.

For the agile and mischievous Jag, this was one of his safe havens, which he used frequently when his actions elicited the anger of some of the bigger local boys or even his family. The very flexible, yet strong branches of the tamarind tree made for very useful whips which were sometimes used to discipline him for his overly curious and naughty actions.

However, way up high among the highest branches, he also found that he was able to weave the slender limbs to form a reclining chair-like structure and as these branches grew, the 'seat' became more comfortable and strong. From this vantage point, he could view most of the surrounding village through the canopy and had a clear line of sight to the ocean beach where the people frolicking in the sand looked like crawling ants. As the tree swayed to the constant silent music of the wind, he found himself mesmerized to sleep in his high hiding spot, finding comfort in the tree limbs cradling his skinny body.

Sometimes when he hid his sister's books or stole some tasty treat from her hiding place in the cupboard they all referred to as the 'safe', he would grab his red 'Craven A' (a brand of cigarettes at the time) shoulder bag with his comic books and scoot up his tree to his 'safe haven' from where he would tease her to 'come and get me'.

But according to some people in his village and neighboring villages there was also a more sinister story to 'his' tree. The whispered word was that the evil and powerful 'Village Master' also inhabited this tree and made it his home, after he had supposedly given up his home on the smaller and older tamarind tree next to the koker. Because of this rumor, many people in the village and the surrounding villages regarded this tree in fear and wanted to do nothing on it or around it. Jag reveled in this story since this meant that not many people tried to encroach onto his personal tree space.

The four to six inch long curved fruit was sour-sweet and legume-like with multiple seeds. The seeds from this fruit were about half inch in size, brown, hard, and shiny and were sometimes used in the place of coins for a childhood games of marbles which was called 'enter-hole'. This was played by making three holes in the dirt about six feet apart with the heel of the foot. The goal was to roll the marble into each hole for a total of nine holes in succession. The first person to complete the nine holes in the minimum number of tries won.

The young, unripe tamarind was eaten with a mix of salt and red peppers. When it was half-ripe the flesh covering the brown seeds was a creamy yellow-green and was also enjoyed with salt and pepper. At fully ripe, the fleshy fruit shrunk away from the shell of a skin. When this shell was cracked open it uncovered the dark brown, sticky, sour-sweet flesh almost drying over the shiny brown seeds and when ripe like this, it was also enjoyed covered in brown sugar.

This tree was one of things in the life of the Mahadeo children's' life which kept them entertained. For Jag this was especially true since his tree kept him safe and out of trouble many times as he grew up.

Jag left for College in 1979. On one of his many visits home, he was very disheartened to find that his friend and favorite tree had been cut down because it was dying. Now, there was just a big, ugly empty spot was in its place and he could not wait to get back to school to escape the harsh reality of his favorite tree now gone.

My Self-Analysis—Poem

I turned around and looked at him
and did not really like what I saw.
He was physically strong and robust,
but his personality had many a flaw.

His voice overflowed with confidence,
Bordering so close to arrogance.
He spoke boldly, with no restraint
. . . showing no humility, not even once.

He knows how to be humble,
Of this I was quite sure.
But he never tries to practice it,
Almost like he remembers no more.

He strode, head high and filled with pride.
With a demeanor that bordered on ego.
The right mix of humility and pride,
This secret, he did not want to know.

He never cultivated any patience
He allowed himself to be aggressive.
Though he was perfectly aware that
this was an unhealthy way to live.

He let himself fall easy prey
to constant and un-suppressed lust.
Although he is surrounded by
Loved ones he knew he could totally trust.

Most-times his anger is under control

And tucked away in it's inside cave.
But sometimes it cunningly escapes him
. . . . and then he becomes his anger's slave.

All these are his major faults,
I will tell him . . . I am a close friend of his.
For I . . . . Am his own conscience,
Performing his Self-Analysis.

Playing Cricket with the Gang

The three Mahadeo brothers came home from school to find that Papa had arrived home a bit early from work. This means that they can all go to the ball field and have fun. Their father always tried to find the time to take them to the ball-field and play with them and encourage them to exercise and be active.

Jag did not like to play cricket with everyone and he would rather be alone with his comic books or to play on his own, but on days like these he especially looked forward to the activities after cricket. His elder brother always tried to encourage him to be a part of the group. Whenever Jag agreed to go with them, his brother always tried to choose him as part of his team whether it was playing cricket or volleyball. He understood why his brother tried to get him involved with the rest of the boys but Jag never felt like he belonged with the group.

Buddy had sent Somesh off on his bicycle to gather the rest of the gang for the game of soft-ball cricket, and within twenty minutes the excited group gathered at the bottom-house. They raced to collect the balls, bats and wickets from behind the kitchen door where they were always kept, then the noisy bunch made their way to the cricket ground. It took just a few minutes to get to the cricket ground, passing by the cemetery on the right. At this time of year, the brown-black water in the little ditch separating the street from the cemetery was alive, jumping and shimmering with what seemed like millions of half-inch long black tadpoles with a thin trailing tail. These would later grow into the big-as-a-hand toads that leaped all over the place and were flattened by traffic on the roads by the hundreds.

The cricket ground (ball-field) was big and square. In the middle of this field was the rectangular flat tamped-hard dirt area called the 'pitch' where one team batted the ball which was 'bowled' by a member of the opposing team. On the north of the ball-field was the cemetery with its big, low shed. A hedge of cactus lined the western boundary. The southern boundary led into an open area beyond which, sat the small Hindu Mandir

111

and then the winding 66 Creek. The back fence of the neighboring yards lined the eastern boundary. Puddles of water filled the small holes trampled in by cattle hooves and a few low lying areas were covered by a shallow sheen of clear rain water from last night's thunderous downpour.

After voting for team captains, the selection of two teams was quickly completed and the game began. Showing true and flexible leadership, Papa coached his eldest son in the art of leading people by emphasizing and encouraging the good plays. For his age Jag was smaller than most of the other boys but he tried to keep up with his older brother's expectations of him. The cricket game lasted about an hour and a half after which they played a game of 'Kabadi' and then 'Coco' which involved a lot of running and shouting. A half hour before dusk they all headed to the sand-reef for a swim, which, for many, was the highlight of the evening.

The sand-reef is part of the drainage system for the rice fields that ran west to east, funneling through a sluice called a 'koker' and emptied into the Corentyne River and the Atlantic Ocean. At high-water, when the sluice gates were closed it was very intimidating, yet a lot of fun. The earth here is of reddish-brown sand from which it derived its local name, and when the water was high it was roughly fifty feet wide, but to the children who did not know how to swim, it looked more like a scary mile-wide. On the north shore of this canal were towering coconut trees that swayed together to the invisible conductor of the wind.

Surrounding the coconut trees was a stand of 'awara' palm trees with its threatening trunk of thorny spikes, and a thick, bushy 'jamoon' tree which beckoned with its grape sized, dark purple fruits which were protected by nests of stinging wasps known locally as 'chasey'. Thick wild 'jamoon' trees which bore small quarter inch purple fruits lined the far side of the canal and the leafy branches lapped delicately at the coffee colored water. To the left of the coconut trees was a swath of prickly briar bush growing at the edge of the water with its thorny branches dipping into the water in rhythm with the gusts of wind swirling over the edge. The scenery was somewhat wild, yet beautiful, inviting and fun.

Those who did not want to make the almost two miles trek to the beach on Sunday mornings came here to swim and pray instead. It was here in this canal known as the 'sand-reef' where most of the neighborhood kids, including Jag, learned to swim. Clumps of floating water grass passed swiftly by in the currents looking like little moving islands, a gift from the rice field drainage canals further inland. They rode the current on their way to the 'koker' and through the raging aqueduct, then finally into the Corentyne river and the ocean. In the minds of the young ones, these clumps of water grasses were scary and harbored evil and horrible creatures, so they stayed as far away as possible from these 'floating islands' as they passed by.

Buoyed by the courage and confidence of his brother Vishwa, his cousin Vimal and the company of the other older boys, Jag pushed aside the fear and joined the rest in the loud, active water games and diving contests. A short while later, exhausted by all the fun of the afternoon, the tired bunch slowly headed home as the blanket of darkness slowly settled around them.

Jag B. Mahadeo

Of Roses and Thorns—Poem

Choices of roses and of thorns,
And of heaven and of hell
Desires of riches and wealth,
Knowing what to keep a secret
. . . . and what to tell

Decisions of what to give and what to take,
And of this life . . . what to make
Choosing between an olive branch
and a lightning rod,
like choosing between the Devil . . . . and God.

Surrendering to hate or to love
Wishing to freely fly . . . . Like a dove.
Weather to stop and listen to the loving heart,
Knowing the heartaches which that can start

Temptations of mental and physical lust
Questions of honesty and of trust
Tolerance of seething anger and of pain
Wishing for sunshine when there is rain

Control of tempting desires and greed,
And of lasting peace . . . . to just plant that seed.
To stay afloat and swim . . . . or slowly sink,
In the face of adversity's wicked wink

Dreams of awesome castles in the air,
And nightmares that awaken us in fear.
Wishing for love-letters on paper of gold,
With love stories worthy to be told.

Acquaintances of whom to be proud
Who only our love would enshroud
What to dispense of and what to hold dear.
And over what, it's worth to shed a tear.

Which fault to show and which to hide?
And which true friends to keep by my side.
At what time which mask should be worn.
These Choices of Roses and of Thorns.

The Raid by GDF Soldiers

The solitude of the night was shredded by the loud, harsh, rumble of the army diesel trucks, and the shrill whine of the Land Rovers as they came to a screaming halt in the middle of the road, in an unnecessary, intimidating show of force. Seconds later came the sounds of trampling boots over the solid, wooden bridge, then the loud demanding call of the soldier in command which was reinforced by the banging of the metal gates with the butt of his rifle.

It was two-forty five in the morning, and Pandit Mahadeo took two soft steps, then cautiously looked out from his dark room through the clear glass, in the middle of the upstairs windows. He saw three army trucks and two army land-rovers unloading dozens of soldiers, armed to the teeth with rifles, pistols, and bayonets. As most of them gathered front of his house, he could see others marching around to the back street where they can get to the back of his home. He waited a full minute until his wife and all his children were awake, and then waited another minute while Mama lit the rest of the kerosene lamps, and Jag lit the kerosene pump-operated lantern. Papa then took a hand lamp and accompanied by Mama and Buddy, they made their way downstairs to open the front door and gate.

While walking down the stairs, he was saying quietly to Mama that this visit was too soon. The soldiers had raided less than a week ago with the excuse of looking for illegal weapons in his house, and the rest of the property. Usually they came once every two weeks and this was cause for concern. Pandit Mahadeo was a high-ranking, highly respected, and influential member of the opposition political party, the People's Progressive Party, (PPP) and these soldiers had orders to make his life and that of his family, very uncomfortable. These searches were done to find some reason or excuse to take him to the police station for questioning and to lock him up in jail.

During these years, the country was in political turmoil. The government was controlled by the People's National Congress, (PNC) and its leader who was a dictator and who kept himself in power by rigging and manipulating the supposedly 'free and fair' elections every five years so that his party always "won". This was despite the fact that popular polls found him to be unwanted and hated as a person and as sorely lacking as a leader. Publicly active members of the People's Progressive Party (PPP) which was the most prominent and influential opposition party, were constantly harassed and jailed in numerous attempts to have them switch sides, or to weaken their will to fight or resist.

About six days ago they came about midnight after a very heavy rain shower. As they always did, they had honored his Papa's request that only seven soldiers do the searching so that a member of his family can stay with each search party. They had inspected every tiny crevice, every closet, and every cupboard and upturned whatever they wanted to at their will. They scoured the backyard, and even had one skinny soldier climb up the shorter coconut trees looking for hidden guns. However, there was always an ulterior motive to these visits. They used these visits to plant guns, explosives, and recording devices in an attempt to pin some type of illegal activity on Mr. Mahadeo. Should they succeed in 'finding' the previously-planted evidence in a subsequent 'search', they would use it as evidence to charge him with possession and have him jailed.

But all these searches were in vain because every weapon or recording device that they ever planted on these 'searching' trips were found immediately after they left by Jag, one of the other siblings, or by Mama and Papa themselves. The frustration was obvious on the soldiers' faces when their subsequent search did not locate the devices or weapons which they had planted on their previous 'searching' visits.

There was one almost comical visit in which the family found much amusement when the soldiers used garden forks to turn up the soil in one 'very suspicious looking', fairly large area, after which Mama thanked them and took the opportunity to plant a bed of tomato plants in the ground which was unwittingly tilled by the soldiers.

But this time around, they did not want to search the house or the yard. As Papa opened the door, the soldier in command, a young man standing at attention, was stern yet respectful as they always were. "Pandit, Mr. Mahadeo, Sir, we have come to search your farm at the reef for illegal weapons and we ask that you come with us". He was surprised that they even knew about his farm at the reef, but Papa answered "Okay, give me a few minutes to get ready".

It was a very dark, moonless night and the stars stuck out brightly, each seemingly trying to outshine the other. On surreal nights like these, the stars seem so close and low, that it felt like one could take a stick and poke the shining crystal beads out of the night sky.

All this unusual activity at this early hour had woken the neighborhood dogs who started complaining to each other in their loud ceaseless barking. This eventually resulted in the whole the village waking up within a few minutes. Soon, the neighbors who were overwhelmed by their curiosity were starting to gather by the roadside.

When it was explained to them that the soldiers intended to take their Pandit, brother, and friend, into the darkness to search his farm, many started to voice their objections loudly since they can imagine the many possible 'accidents' that can happen to their much-loved Pandit and brother, away from the presence of anyone else. It was quickly decided among the villagers that many of them will accompany Pandit and the search party to the farm. The soldiers at first objected to the suggestion, but eventually, they reluctantly gave in.

Three long, sleepless, and nervous hours later, with some of the neighbors waiting up with the rest of the Mahadeo family, the search party of soldiers along with Papa returned muddy and tired from their long trek in the dark. A few of them now itching, and sporting scratches on their arm and faces from the bushes which must have objected to their night intrusion.

As Papa related later, the soldiers had made a beeline for the drum of illegal explosives they had themselves planted on Pandit Mahadeo's farm many days ago. However, this planted item had been found and removed the previous day. A few days ago, Jag was roaming in the bushes as he usually does looking for wild fruits, and he came across a four inch diameter hole in the red sand which seemed to have been washed in from the recent rains. He took a sturdy stick and poked at the hole and it collapsed further to reveal a bluish plastic drum, buried about a foot beneath the surface of the sand. He went to his father and explained his find and later, in the secret of night, his father and a few others had dug out the drum, and floated it down river.

Events like these only resulted in a stronger Mahadeo family. The five children grew up proud, strong and fearless in the face of constant intimidation. They grew up weary, yet prepared and confident. These experiences made them tough-minded, resilient, and committed to the same morals, which their father and mother followed and lived throughout their lives.

The raids by the soldiers continued for many, many years and every single search ended the same way. In frustration for the soldiers who came with the intention of finding a reason to take Pandit Mahadeo into custody and keeping him jailed for a long time.

The Beast in me—Poem

In the deep recesses of my being,
There is a monstrous beast in me.
Hidden and disguised so very well,
Hard for anyone else outside to see

Locked up and tucked away,
In one of my mind's many cages
He cannot control my body,
Even in his constant manic rages.

He constantly begs for my attention,
He pleads "let me out please".
Even though he is my life's companion,
Him, I will do nothing to appease.

I will tell you of my terrible beast,
And the things he is capable of.
He is so much like my own twin,
But he is incapable of showing love.

He is the selfish bigot in me.
He is the one who constantly lusts.
He is the braggart and the showoff.
He cares not about righteous or just.

He is selfish and he is downright mean,
And he listens when the devil beckons.
This is why I am on guard against him
Every day and every single second

You see, he is the one who gets angry,

So furious sometimes, he can kill.
I cannot give him any bit of control,
Or he will cause great havoc at his will.

He makes me scream, yell and curse,
He gets violent, rant and rave.
If I listen to him, I don't belong here,
I should be living in a far away cave.

Constant thinking, he always does,
For he never ever goes to sleep
Make me do mean things to those I love,
The things that make them hurt and weep.

This is why he is always locked up,
And bound with chains oh-so-strong
So he never ever escapes or breaks out,
To take control and do his wrongs

Even though I keep him securely under wraps,
I've tried . . . but never could silence him.
I will stay in the saddle and keep the reins tight,
So he can never satisfy his whim.

So, I have a terrible beast in me,
But his things, he never ever gets to do.
Don't you even think of mocking me
For you have your beast in you too.

Lesson in Discipline

They sat together on the veranda, watching the bustling activities at the decrepit-looking saw-mill across the road, by the edge of the wide murky waters of the wide Berbice River. The machinery noises undulated with the gusting wind, which also swept the pungent scent of fresh cut timber to their nostrils. The thick overgrowth of deep, green vegetation along the edge of the river kept some areas secret, but next to the saw-mill a few large ships could be seen sailing to the loading docks further upriver.

Their father, in addition to being a Pandit, a politician, and a rice farmer, was also the manager of Continental Agency Company in the town of New Amsterdam, at the mouth of the Berbice River, forty miles north of their home in the village. The company was a distributor of many consumable items including candies, (mints, gums, lollipops, etc.) paints, varnishes, and many other household products. The offices of Continental Agency were located in the lower level of this building, and the large extended warehouse took up the rest of the yard in the back. During the work week, his father lived in the upper level which was relatively well furnished compared to their house at No. 66 Village.

This was the only getaway which the children had and they took advantage of it whenever their father allowed them. This week, he and his sister Shanie who he called 'Lil', spent the week here and had a lot of fun away from home. This was also another place where the inquisitive little boy found himself in a lot of trouble. It was here where, for the first time, they first saw a telephone, and it was only a matter of time before they found themselves tempted by its functions. His young mind was fascinated with this new fangled device and together with his sister; they spent many hours confounding the phone operator by picking up the phone, saying 'hello', and hanging up when someone answered. This eventually prompted the frustrated operator to trace the phone number and then alerting his father about the abuse. Both of them were summoned into their father's office and it was with much apprehension that the two slowly made their way downstairs into the large office and stood before their father. At first, they both denied any wrongdoing and after a lengthy discussion, Jag tried to pass the blame to his sister, loudly denying being guilty of anything. But his father knew him very well and recognized the signs which told him that Jag was indeed guilty. Once again, he had his bottom spanked for his naughtiness.

This was also the first time he had seen a refrigerator, and he and his sister had fun poking around it, trying to figure out whether the light stays on after the door is closed, what made the humming sound and where exactly the freezing cold came from. They tried to freeze everything and soon after, he again found himself in trouble for purposely putting bottles of 'Red Spot' orange soda into the freezer, so that he could eat the frozen slush when the bottle cracked and broke apart in the extreme cold.

In the warehouse, the two spent many fun hours roaming around, playing and satisfying their curiosity. They spent hours watching and learning how to use the paint mixing machine, and watching the workers move stuff around with pallet jacks. To their delight, they soon found that they could 'accidentally' poke holes in the plastic bags of candies, and eat the goodies from the broken bags without getting caught. Many of the bags actually broke in handling, and it was hard to distinguish which ones were broken on purpose.

Mama and their baby brother Yog had come from the village the previous morning and they spent the day enjoying Mama's cooking and in the evening, shopping with her. The next day was Saturday and as usual, the biggest market day of the week. After breakfast, they all went to the New Amsterdam market which was a cross between an open air and closed stalls market and much bigger than the Skeldon Market which they visited at home. It was extremely hot and humid, as they moved among the throngs of people navigating their way among the selections, which on display at each stall. The heavy, overpowering smell, from the fish and meat area of the market assaulted the senses of the strict vegetarian family and while covering their noses or holding their breath, they quickly made their way through this uncomfortable part of the market.

As the setting sun started dipping beyond the rushing waters of the Berbice River, they were all packed and ready to leave for home in the village. The four gathered in the back of the house to watch Papa, who, with the help of one of his workers, cut down a bunch of ripe bananas from the giant banana plant growing next to the house. This banana plant was one of the biggest they had ever seen and the bunch of bananas was huge. Two thirds of this huge bunch was placed on rice bags in the trunk of his father's car to be taken home for the family.

Half an hour into the ride home, while fidgeting in the back seat with his sister, it was discovered that Jag had taken a small box of ball-point pens from the warehouse, without permission. His father, who held honesty and trust in the highest regard, was very upset. He stopped the car in an area known as '19 Village' which had a very straight, dark, and desolate stretch of road a few miles past the toll booth. It seemed like Papa was always admonishing his second son about his bad habits but he never seem to learn.

A week ago he was spanked for cutting the seat cushions of Papa's car with a razor blade. Papa and Mama spent some time with him after the usual spanking, trying to explain to him why he must change his behavior. When asked to explain his reasons for cutting the car seats, he explained that he was fascinated by the long, shiny threads of all colors, which were embedded in the stuffing material of the car seats. He had reached underneath and pulled as much of it as he could get, then when he could not get any more from beneath the seat, he resorted to cutting the seats to get more of the shiny threads.

But this time, Papa was very angry and was determined to teach his son a hard lesson. He told Jag that his actions were very dishonest and unacceptable and he cannot ride in the same car with his honest family. He told him that he should walk home from here and use the time while walking, to think about his unacceptable behavior. He explained that he knew that his son was a good boy, who needs to control his bad habits and that he should think before doing anything. Mama however, disagreed with the form of punishment but Papa insisted on delivering the hard lesson.

They were about thirty miles from home and the little boy was very scared of this pitch black area. On the western side of the road were towering sugarcane plants stretching for miles. In his mind the wind unimpeded by any trees around, seemed to howl and hiss through the cane fields. On the eastern side of the road, the flooded area which was a few miles long was used as a fish farm. There were no houses anywhere nearby. The closest house was a few miles away. The darkness echoed with the shrill noises of the night insects and other creatures that croaked, howled and hissed. Jag was scared stiff but was determined not to show it.

Young as he was, he had a lot of pride and quite a hot temper, and now he angrily stalked away heading south, in the direction of home. The rest of the family watched him walking away for a few long minutes, then at Papa's urging, climbed back into the car and they drove off, passing by the boy who had made little progress. While walking, he looked for and picked up a big muddy stick which he used as a walking stick, but more importantly, he carried it with him in case he was attacked by dogs or other animals as he walked. The sounds of the night here was unlike anything he had heard before. Strange and unknown creatures jumped in the broad expanse of water on the left, making 'plunk-plunk' noises, and he moved more to the center of the road as he walked. The wind moving through the cane hissed and roared, as thousands of large leaves and stalks shuffled and brushed against each other in a vain attempt to resist the forceful wind.

He had covered maybe a half of a mile when he saw headlights approaching and not wanting to take any chances, he moved to the side of the road and crouched down. The car passed by and he saw that it was his Papa. He stood up and he kept on walking, angry that they had deserted him. Papa completed a U-turn and came up behind him and his mother pleaded with him to get back into the car.

Days later his sister 'Lil' confided to him that Papa had stopped the car a mile away and they waited a while with the lights off, then turned back to pick him up after a few minutes.

The sternness and patience of his father, the severity of these lessons over a period of time, and the love with which Mama encouraged Jag, eventually won out and he took these lessons to heart. He was starting to become very conscious of the decisions he made, and was beginning to think before acting on his impulses, which got him into so much trouble. He understood that his father and mother just wanted the best for him and wanted him to become a good person so that he could find his happiness in his life

On 'Trust'
Every person on earth is part of your family. Do not distrust everyone until they give you a reason to trust them.
Instead, trust everyone until someone gives you a reason not to trust them.
                                        Pandit Budhram Mahadeo (Papa)

2001

The Funeral Pyre—Poem

Circling in the blue sky way up high,
I noticed this great commotion down below.
Hundreds of people filed slowly along.
What's going on down there? This I have got to know.

So I swiftly flew lower down
so I can see whatever will transpire.
I saw this great dry stack of wood
That was set up and formed as a funeral pyre.

Waves of people walked to this open space
and solemnly they gathered around,
and started a chant to the heavens.
O such a hauntingly, beautiful sound.

Then the chanting came to a stop
A sword of calmness sliced the air.
A quiet of a deeply solemn mood
broken only by a cry here and there.

Then a body from a wooden platform
Gently placed on top the pyre!
I now can see the ultimate plan!
That human body they will set afire?

The throng finally settled down.

Many were dressed in all white.
And were crying out so painfully loud,
That I wondered at their terrible plight.

Circling up here on tired wings,
I should find a place to stop and sit.
That tall tree by the pavilion looks just right.
From that height I will observe every bit.

From my perch, now I surveyed the scene,
One bearded young man took the lead.
They started the chanting and singing again,
On the pyre they spread herbs and seeds.

A small fire was set ablaze on one side
then in ritual, shared to the other three.
It was so packed and crowded around there.
It was getting very difficult to see.

So I took off on my tired wings again
And flew over this busy, crowded space.
I can see through the top layer of wood
The figure laid out in its final resting place.

The chanting grew louder in pitch and
into the fire handfuls of herbs were thrown.
The mournful loud chanting and singing
Intermingled with occasional cries and moans.

A lady dressed in white was singing really loud
and around her a crying group gathered close.
From among this close-knit family group
the loudest singing, chants and cries arose.

Then when the wood pyre caught the heat
and the licking flames quickly, hungrily, spread,
The whole crowd joined in loud singing
as the final Vedic prayers were read.

I flew back to the top of my tall green tree.
The crackling flames grew high and then silence fell
What was on that close family's mind?
I seemed that only the Great God could tell.

The minutes turned to hours and many left.
The group in white retreated under a small tree.
The people still sitting in the pavilion
Stayed right there and just let them be.

There was a long solemn silence
Except for a few muffled sobs here and there.
The greedy red flames were roaring high
And thin wind-swept smoke filled the air.

They sat around for hours . . . . all cried out,
then slowly, tiredly, packed up to go.
Now the fire was mostly bright glowing embers,
Burnt and crumbled down, and quite low.

They all got into a small blue van and went away.
Left the crackling embers still glowing red.
I think, tonight I will roost right here.
In this comfortable tree I will make my bed.

The next morning was so beautiful and still.
The blazing sun rose bright and sharp.
The little group came back at around eleven
bringing buckets, mallets and a big blue tarp.

This they stretched and hung over the spot
Where yesterday the funeral pyre was.
Ceaseless and loud things were heard underneath.
This busy little group was busy and abuzz.

They were digging, searching and washing,
Talking, sweeping and scratching.

On one side, on a cement block,
they took turns pounding and smashing.

When the tarp finally came down I was amazed.
The entire site was washed and picked clean.
All the gray fire ashes were packed in buckets.
On the pyre site, not a bit could be seen.

The somber group packed up into the blue van
And once again they all went away.
What strange human things I've seen
these past few long days.

Then through the whisperings of my fellow souls
I finally learned at last
It was the funeral and last rites of
the Great Pandit Budhram Mahadeo
who had passed.

Finding Our Dog Rio

It had rained all week, and Mama saw this as a good opportunity for the planting of small vegetable seedlings in the garden on the creek-dam. On wet consecutive days like these, the seedlings would take root and not be beaten down by the hot sun. If they did not take this opportunity to plant them, the seedlings will then have to be protected from the sun by little tent-like structures which they would have to build from bushy branches, so that the harsh sun does not burn the seedlings.

Mother and son left home covered by two four-foot square plastic sheets and carrying the little plants tied in careful bunches, they headed for the back-dam four and a half miles away. It was a very slippery walk to the farm. To avoid slipping and falling, Jag was encouraged to use the pigeon toed walk which was done using the toes to get toe holds in the soft, slippery ground while walking. The incessant croaking of the frogs and large toads which were still invisible, seemed to echo on and on, and peaked in a chorus of loud snorts as the toad 'voices' overlapped every so often.

Ahead of them a few fishermen can be seen in the distance throwing their nets into the 'side-line' canal to catch fish. For many of these men this was a way to get a meal to feed their family, or to make a living by selling the fish they caught. Along the way, Mama and her son stopped to throw back the unwanted fishes which were left stranded, gasping and thrashing about, among the short grasses along the side of the dam. These consisted of little silver fishes called 'potya', the 'loco-loco', an eel type pink fish which was between six inches and a foot long, and many others. Acts like these, of kindness, tenderness, consideration for all living things, and the explanations provided by his mother along the way, helped the young boy to understand the importance of life and the importance of different creatures in Mother Nature's garden.

As they walked, swarms of mosquitoes tried to seek shelter under their plastic covers and they had to pull the sheets close to their faces and sometimes run to escape the persistent, dark, clouds of insects. Under the gray overcast sky and the constant light spritz of rain, they reached their rice fields an hour and a half later. After adjusting the drainage 'cut' to drain away the excess rain water, the two walked through the rice field, inspecting the plants for diseases. Then they went to the 'creek-dam' where they spent the next four hours planting the little seedlings with the pouring rain beating down upon them.

Their other five acres of rice land was directly across from them, on the other side of the 66 Creek. Jag did not know how to swim well as yet and the currents were strong, so around noon they made their way back to the main trail and started walking another half a mile to the 'cross-line dam'. This trail took them around the 'cross-line dam' which bridged the creek by a concrete footpath that stretched over the aqueduct koker (picture) as a twelve inch wide moss-covered, rough, concrete beam. Under this 'bridge', the black, tea-colored, savannah waters rushed by in a noisy, bubbling, tumbling torrent, the roiling water rolling upon itself, frothing white like some great, hungry monster. From here, it raced on it way to mix with the brown silt-laden waters of the Corentyne River.

Except for a narrow and muddy, much-used trail, this entire area was overgrown with ten feet tall 'moko-moko' plants and vines which encroached over everything almost like it was trying to strangle and smother every living thing in the area. Jag had the scary thought that if someone was to stand still for a few minutes, the threatening vines would actually grow over him. There were also huge clumps of briar, and the 'shame-baby' plant which sported it own defense of thorns. This 'shame-baby' plant came by its local name of 'shame-baby' because when something touched the multi-leafed fronds, the leaves closed up in defense until they resembled small stems.

The only bare ground in this area was the muddy trail which was torn up by the feet of animals. For Jag, it was a very scary crossing and though apprehensive, he refused to show any fear. With his mother watching carefully, and holding his arms wide from under the loose, flapping, plastic sheet covering him, he slowly made his way over the aqueduct.

As he waited for his mother to cross the bridge of the concrete beam, a small puppy about twelve inches high walked out from the bushes next to his mother, crying and whimpering. He was a cute tan brown, with black ear tips, and a black nose. He was wet, cold, shaking, and whining in fear. As his mother turned to look at the puppy, Jag scared his mother by running back over the twelve inch wide concrete beam in excitement, when she was not looking.

In her tender, loving way, Mama picked up the mud covered puppy and sat down, held him close to her and spoke softly in his ear, which made the puppy calm down and slowly relax. She came to the conclusion that the puppy was left behind by someone who crossed over the aqueduct earlier, and that maybe he wanted to cross over the bridge too. She held him gently under her left arm and covered his eyes with her right hand to prevent him from seeing the rushing water beneath and squirming in fear. If he did this it could cause her to lose her own balance. Now she slowly crossed over the narrow bridge and gently put him down.

Five minutes later, they stopped at the far side of the cross-line dam to take their lunch from the little 'sauce-pan' which his mother had packed from home. Both ate their lunch using the broad leaves of the 'wild-starch' plant (a plant much like the Canna-lily) as plates and the God-given forks of their fingers. Lunch included rice and fried bigan with hot green bird peppers which Mama had picked from the bushes close by. Lunch was washed down with the sweet fresh 'black' water from the aqueduct nearby. After they tenderly fed the starving puppy some of their food, he stared at them adoringly, jumping up and down in joy, his long, thin, black-tipped tail swinging wildly from side to side. Jag begged his mom to keep the puppy to which she responded that "if his owner does not show up to claim him, we will keep him".

While his mother picked more wild bird peppers and 'moko-moko' flowers to take home, Jag picked handfuls of the wild fig-like fruit known locally as Paakhar to eat on the long trek home. These half-inch diameter fruits were soft and juicy and his mother showed him how to string them onto the long blades of grass, until they resemble necklaces of little reddish-brown marbles. Later as they walked he would pull them off the 'strings' with his mouth and happily chomp on them. This usually kept him entertained for a good part of the journey home.

They walked on carefully, skirting around the huge sand-koker trees which discarded very sharp, tack-shaped thorns from their branches. For some reason, just a tiny prick on the feet with these thorns burned painfully, and they both avoided them as much as they could. After another half-hour with the puppy following close behind, they arrived at their second five-acre of rice field where they checked on the plants for any diseases, and made sure that the water level was just right.

By the time they arrived home it was dark. Jag and Mama carefully gave the little puppy a bath to wash off all the caked mud, which had dried onto his furry body. Then they dried him off with an old towel. Now clean, the puppy pranced around showing off his now shiny, light-brown coat. Jag was so excited about the beautiful little puppy now in their midst, that he could not sleep for a long time that night.

From that moment on, Rio, as they had named the energetic puppy, never left Jag's side and accompanied him everywhere. Now a full grown dog, Rio even followed him to the Mandir on Sundays, where he would wait under the church (which was built on stilts, about four feet off the ground) until everyone came out. Then with tail wagging and his face lighting up in happiness, he would search out Jag and they would walk back home together.

A few years later when the boy in his early teens, started to go to the back-dam and tending to the rice fields and vegetable garden by himself, Rio his dog, was his constant, playful companion, protecting him from the other animals, following his every step, swimming the streams with him, and running swiftly alongside his bike for mile after tireless mile. Rio was the true alpha dog and when going to the farms, he always acted like the world and everything in it, belonged to him and he was afraid of absolutely nothing. On one memorable trip to the farm Rio started barking and tormenting the lead bull in a small herd of cattle until the bull had enough of him and angrily charged at him. Rio retreated next to Jag and kept up his fierce verbal argument with the huge bull, which made the bull even angrier. The bull pawed the ground and put on a fearsome display of wild snorting and romping, then charged after both the boy and the dog. Jag had no choice but to try and escape the bull by plunging in and swimming over the high brown water of the side-line canal. When Rio turned around and realized that he was now all alone against the bull, he took one giant running leap over the canal, making it over the two foot bordering grasses and halfway across the canal, then swam the rest of the way to the other side. After his desperate, maddening plunge into the water, he quieted down and the two walked in the direction of home among the high grass. The bull followed for a while but since the dog was no longer barking, he finally gave up the chase.

One of the saddest day of Jag's life happened many years later when, because of his constant, watchful vigil, and unforgiving policing of Pandit Mahadeo's yard, Rio the loyal and fun family dog died as a result of poisoning by unknown persons of cruel, evil, and unexplainable motivations.

That miserable morning of sorrow, before the sun came up, Mama and Jag heard Rio whimpering and ran downstairs to find him laid out flat, breathing very shallow, and body writhing stiffly, with deep pain in his sad eyes. They did not know what to do, so they gave him water and tried to make him comfortable. Jag was heartbroken and crying and Rio stared at Jag and his mother with adoring eyes and his proud mouth moved in slow motion, almost like he was trying to tell them something. Very slowly, those sad, beautiful eyes closed, with mother and son watching and cradling his head and body. With one last, slow breath, Rio passed away leaving the two feeling very lonely, heartbroken and sad.

Later that same day, with the boy still crying uncontrollably, he and his mother dug a three feet long, two feet wide and three feet deep hole in front of the small tamarind tree in the back yard. (A seedling of the big tamarind tree) Wrapping the cold, now-stiff body in the rice bag which was used as his favorite sleeping mat, they put Rio's body in its final resting place. With a heavy heart, they covered it with dirt, one sad shovelful after another as the rain slowly started falling as if Mother Nature herself was in tears for her child Rio.

To this day, every time Jag visits his childhood home, he takes his wife Dee and two children Avi and Vashti next to the now grown tamarind tree and spend a few moments remembering the good times with his unforgettable childhood friend, his fun and loving dog Rio.

Under the Tamarind Tree—Poem

Little Boy sobbing and slowly digging
Three feet deep, three feet long
Two feet wide
One long-handled shovel,
Gripped in calloused little old looking hands
Sweating and clawing at the unforgiving, damp clay.
Digging
Pushing
Digging
Fighting back the flow of tears
Dripping from red, swollen, cry-weary eyes
Pants tattered and muddy
Bony knees skinned and bleeding
Wrapping the body of his beautiful
Brown friend in his favorite burlap sack
He gives it one last aching hug
And puts the cold, stiff carcass down
Thud!
His little heart fell into the hole with it.
Tenderly raking loose earth over the dreaded hole,
Earth with tear-soaked brownish-gray spots
He covers it gently even in death.
His poor dog . . . . his best friend.
Now dead
Buried under the Tamarind tree
Feeling so very lonely
Little Boy alone
And heartbroken
He hugs his mother in tears.

Our New Car

Pandit Mahadeo had bought a new car a few years ago in 1966. It was a small beautiful thing, a light sky-blue Morris Minor, and it was perfect just for the Mahadeo family. Its silhouette was highlighted by its two prominent front fenders, each of which could comfortable seat a small person. These were complemented by the smaller rear fenders from which the red, chrome-ringed housing of the rear lights protruded. At this time, aside from the 'hire' cars (taxies) it was one of the few private cars in the neighboring villages. It had a light blue leatherette interior and instrument panel that was primarily a large round centrally mounted speedometer.

Around the periphery of this speedometer was a chrome plated ring, which the little boy delighted in polishing and watching it as got shinier when the haze which accumulated over the hot, humid days succumbed to his efforts. As their father arrived home from his job, daily political meetings or religious sermons, the sound of the little car's distinctive horn would send them all racing to be the first to open the gate, so their Papa could drive into the 'bottom-house'. For a while this competition between the children continued until the excitement and newness of the car wore out.

Each morning Papa would open the car 'bonnet' hood, engage the black metal elbow prop that kept the hood open, then check the engine oil, brake fluid, battery fluid and radiator water level of his car. Since his eldest son Vishwa, who everyone referred lovingly to as 'Buddy' was now about fourteen years old, Papa decided that his son was responsible enough to do this daily check for him.

One early July morning, while his father was upstairs getting ready to leave for work, Buddy opened the car bonnet to check the engine oil and other fluids. He could hear his sister Shanie sweeping and cleaning upstairs. His mother was in the kitchen preparing breakfast and looking after his younger brother Yog, who was just six years old. The Kiskadees were singing the sweet, early morning version of their 'kis-ka-dee-kis-kis-ka-dee' song, and the two blackbirds who insisted on making their nest in the rafters of the 'bottom-house' were arguing over the one egg which fell and shattered on the ground, leaving only a small damp spot, of oily yellow and white. Above the car in the rafters, the colony of mahogany colored wasps known locally as 'marabuntas' were busy rebuilding their paper-thin nests once again.

Instead of killing the insects, these fragile nests, sometimes housing the eggs or baby insects, were always knocked down in an effort to convince the wasps go build them somewhere else, but they loved the protected area of the 'bottom-house' and insisted on coming back and rebuilding their nests here. This 'game' of breaking and rebuilding continued over the years.

The small hibiscus plant which grew against the front fence and sported dozens of pink-red flowers was having its daily visitor, a small hummingbird who stopped and hovered magically in front of each flower for a few seconds, flitting back and forth silently.

As his brother checked the car fluids, Jag, who was annoyingly inquisitive, hung around peering at the engine, touching everything he could reach with his small hands and pestered his elder brother with questions. With his typical patience in everything he did, Buddy showed him and explained what he knew about all the 'stuff' under the hood of the car. Then as Buddy leaned over to pull out the dipstick to check the oil level, Jag hit the prop which kept the bonnet up to see what would happen, and watched in surprise and dismay as the bonnet collapsed and hit Buddy in the middle of his head with a dull 'thud'. Buddy slowly pulled himself out from under the bonnet with blood flowing freely down his face and over his nose. Jag's spirits sank. He felt miserable at what he had done and he was now frozen in shock. Mama, looking out of the open kitchen window saw the blood and came running out. When he saw his Mama approaching to tend to her eldest son's injury, Jag sprung into action, grabbed an empty bag to use as a mat and took off for one of his hiding spots.

In the backyard fifty feet from the house, all the way to the left, there grew three huge cherry trees with dense, deep green foliage about ten feet high, and so close together that they looked like one tree, with their lower branches drooping down to the fertile black soil. When in season, the branches of these trees are laden with cherries to the point of breakage. To pick these cherries, Mama would spread rice bags under the trees and together with the children; shake the branches to collect the cherries in the bags. With the bucketful of bright red cherries, Mama would lovingly prepare a pot of cherry jam which her children, especially Jag, loved to eat with roti.

Months ago between these branches and the main trunks of the trees, he had moved and intertwined the flexible stems to create a tunnel-like space about four feet wide, eight feet long, and high enough to sit up and move around. He liked it here, with the wild sweet smells which wafted in the gentle breeze every so often. On this day, the air was fragrant with the scent of a wild white flower growing on a vine that threatened to smother the backside of the cherry trees, and the sweet smell of rotting 'sapodilla' fruits in the neighbor's yard, which hung enticingly in the still air.

Now he laid chest down on the rice bag, while the vision of his brother's bloody face kept flashing before his eyes. He felt terribly guilty as the horror of what had happened, sunk into his brain. His heart pounded loudly in his chest and against the hard earth. He had not expected that the car bonnet would come down so fast, and hit his brother so hard, and he dreaded facing his father after this incident. He will certainly be punished again for being bad.

But his mother was very loving and understanding. She did not want to see her husband upset at Jag this early in the morning, or to see Jag once again be punished for his consistently naughty actions. So she quietly brought Buddy around back to the outdoor fireside area of the kitchen, while his father got into his car and drove off to work without knowing what had transpired. Now she gently tended to Buddy's wound, parting his thick black hair, and washing his scalp carefully, using coconut oil on his lacerations and devising a crude bandage to keep it clean.

Next, she went to the backyard, and not knowing where Jag was, called out to him. She said "Jag my son; I know you did not mean to hurt your brother. It's okay. Come on inside and eat your sugar roti. You won't be punished"

But Jag was still very upset at himself. He waited a while before sneaking into the kitchen and without saying a word to anyone; he sat down in a corner of the kitchen table, and finished his sugar-roti and his tea. After he was done he washed up, quietly took his bag of comic books, and went back to his hiding spot where he spent the rest of the day grateful that his mother had once again saved him from punishment

Out! Out! Out I Say—Poem

Peering through the layers of fog,
Into the mirror of my mind
The little storm has become a raging tempest.
Violent, destructive, and quite unkind!
Emotions stirred and tossed and turned.
Unseen tears . . . . angry, turbulent rivers!
Outward peace and calmness only betrayed
By shaky voice from lips that quivered.

But . . .!

I shall not be the helpless driftwood
At the mercy of every passing ripple
I shall not be the cotton-ball cloud
At the whim of ever-changing winds
I shall not be the broken-hearted lover.
Loving genuine love . . . . but still unloved.
And I shall not be the dancing puppet
At the end of a set of moving strings
. . . .

No! It shall not be!
So now, you hear this!

Out! Out! Out I say!
You are not welcomed in my mind today.
I cannot entertain you, so get out of my mind.
You are no good for me . . . . and not too kind.

You are just an addiction to which I was bound.
Now I resist, but still see your shadows all around.

Please take all my thoughts of you when you go,
And make it a bit easier for me to say no.

With all my time I shall do better things,
And not suffer the pains your presence brings.
No longer shall I shed tears for your sake.
This mistake again and again, I shall not make.

Step through my mind's door and I shall push you out.
You and all your troubles, I can do without.
I shall close my door and not open at your knock.
To you, my heart and will . . . . Shall be a rock.

So, you keep your damned bottle and your pill.
As of today, me, you shall not kill.
So! Out! Out! Out I say!
You are not welcomed in my mind today.

Buying Contraband

In his mind, he was on a very scary and dangerous mission. His mother has sent him to buy contraband goods.

In the years 1973 to 1978 the dictatorship that ruled Guyana under the PNC led by Forbes Burnham, banned most food staples used primarily by one segment of the Guyanese society, those of East Indian decent. Items which were once taken for granted were no longer available. On the banned list were potato, chick peas, split peas, onion, garlic, wheat flour, cheese, barley, oats, tomato paste and many others. This led to a period of suffering, malnutrition, illegal trade, and also innovation, where the people had to use their imagination and skill to come up with new ways of making nutritious and tasty meals using only locally grown foods, ingredients, home-made concoctions and recipes.

Mama had tasked him, told where to go, and insisted on him being very careful that no one noticed him. But the Mahadeo children were used to being careful. Their father, Pandit Budhram Mahadeo is constantly teaching his five children how to take precautions wherever they went. When among others, like on the busy road or at the open market, they knew to be careful of what people have in their hands around them. In any situation, they were taught to be careful and aware of their surroundings. The opposition party and those who were against his father can try to hurt his father through hurting his children so they were all taught how to be very observant and cautious. At home they knew how not to walk between the lamp and the window, where a shadow cast upon the window can betray their position in the house to someone who may have bad intentions. When coming out of their home or out of any other building, they were taught to look around for any suspicious activity or persons. Papa was always teaching them boxing and how to defend themselves and to wrestle and he always found a way to make this kind of education a bit of fun for his children.

Papa taught them well and though young, Jag was very confident. He was on an errand to buy 'illegal' potatoes or 'aaloo' as it was locally known.

If the police found anyone with contraband items, they would be jailed and have to pay fines. The items and vehicles used in the transportation of them were also seized. Jag did not want his bike seized or to be jailed and he was a bit nervous. It was approaching darkness when, with an assumed air of bravado to disguise his fear, he did a running horse mount of his bicycle, (where one would run very fast pushing the bike and then jump astride the seat) and took off pedaling furiously to Number 65 Village. At the 'koker' a barking dog, black as the night, raced behind him keeping pace, while exposing to everyone the presence of the secretive little boy on the oversized bicycle. He rode into the east side 'koker' street, a rough clay-packed and bumpy surface, the center of which rose about four feet higher than the rest, as an earthen dyke to protect the village from the occasional extra-high tides. He rode fast, braking with his feet, and his rear tire skidded while making the left turn into the somewhat wider street going north. A few hundred feet farther he rode through the gates of the house where the smuggled goods were being sold.

Money was exchanged for the 'aaloo' almost in total darkness, for there was the constant fear of discontented neighbors turning the seller over to the police, which would then result in the police raiding the home of the buyer and the seller. The people who lived here were the secondary 'distributors' of the contraband goods.

Those who actually risked their lives to bring all these grocery items from the neighboring country of Suriname were the ones who took the most risks. In the blackness of night, they used their small fishing boats to make stealthy, nightly trips to bring the banned goods to sell to the people in the villages. Both docking and loading sites were based in deeply wooded areas of the shores since this type of trade were illegal in both countries. To add to the danger, they were preyed upon by sea pirates who, if they were caught by them, stole all their possession and sometimes sunk their boats. Many of these young men who plied this trade where maimed or killed by pirates. Bags, boxes, and crates of these items were carried on the backs of these young men from the beaches and through the many secret footpaths in the deep mud from the meandering '66 creek'.

Now, with the transaction complete, the young boy cautiously pushed his bike loaded with the plastic bag of potatoes hanging from the handlebar, out of the gate to the street, looking around to make sure that he was still unseen. When he felt safe, he jumped aboard and sped off for the safety of home, once again speeding by the dog that was waiting for him to pass by, barking like mad and following him for about one hundred feet before finally giving up the chase by the koker. Here Jag stopped to watch the sluice operator as he slowly hand-cranked the gears which raised the two large black painted gates. Opening these gates released the surge of high, muddy water, waiting to race to the waiting, welcoming ocean. He listened to the clanging of metal gears as the water started flowing, first as a slow quiet trickle which eventually rose into a noisy din as the brown water frothed and boiled in its freedom to escape from its land-bound prison.

When he arrived home the 'aaloo' was immediately hidden in the back yard among the bushes. Here, if the soldiers were to find it, it would not be in the house and it could be told that anyone could have thrown it there. He breathed a sigh of relief. Mission accomplished! Now he looked forward to eating 'aaloo' curry, which was a rare treat in those days.

Ashes Sown To The Wind—Poem

Dead! Your ashes sown to the wind!
Only fleeting memories in moments of discord.
All the hurt and painful compulsions buried,
with all the weight of guilt they carried.

You; Thief of endless nights of sleep.
Conquering invader of my thoughts.
You; cruel, loudly mocking jackal.
Laughing at the mind battles we fought.

Like a snake slithering into my dreams,
Hissing at even any hint of a smile
And disguising your heartless, gruesome self
as my pure, angel savior once in a while.

And through hidden fangs that tasted of honey
poisoned my mind . . . . in an effort to rule.
My warped perspective, your mind-bending charm,
and into your trap I fell . . . . A complete fool.

Then your familiar embrace threatened my soul
crushing my sanity, leaving me self-less.
Of your compulsions I could not resist.
That you almost succeeded, I must confess.

Then one day I awoke and searched in my mind.
And in the confusion, could not find the real ME.
Among my thoughts, dreams, disguises and beliefs,
only your influence, infestation and poison I see.

So I took a chance on a secret oath that day

that you I will destroy, you I will kill.
And return my mind's real-estate to me,
And in it's throne re-establish my own self-will.

So each of my thoughts I carefully unwrapped
and threw your glittering poison-wrappings away.
Wiped my worthy thoughts clean and kept you out,
and with that very act, you I began to slay.

Carefully now, I nurtured my golden-garden mind,
and enjoyed my new found freedom to think.
I felt revived, in control, a pleasure it is,
to no longer breathe in your poison-stink.

Now you're dead, your ashes sown to the wind.
Your fleeting memories no longer pass by.
No more poison, anxiety, and no more pain.
Not since that day when I watched you die.

Be Still Dear Heart—Poem

I cannot control it. It's over. It's done.
Fretting and agonizing will help none.
Now stop and help me gather my wits.
And put back together my shattered bits.

Calm down, my tender, fragile, fluttering friend.
Feel the new beginning and forget the past end.
Beat back the tide of yesterday's surging wave.
And savor the ensuing stillness . . . . for you will be safe.

Contemplate and endure the aftermath,
and you'll be spared the Devil's own wrath.
Stand tall, be humble, but do not beg.
Face your adversities . . . . even on a bad leg.

Dwell not on that, which might have been,
and be spared all that, better left unseen.
Close your mind's door to the insidious ways.
Open your windows to hopefully brighter days.

Numb yourself to the agony of warped hell.
And keep the raging raucous outside thy shell
through the constant pounding you'll feel no pain,
so brave lion pull yourself up, by your generous mane.

And show your formidable strength . . . . be not timid!
Of these weak emotions, you'll soon be rid.
Because, of something powerful, this is a start,
So behave, be peaceful and be still Dear Heart.

Dr. Cheddi Jagan's Visit

Since hours before dawn, the Mahadeo household was abuzz with continuous activity in the kitchen. Now at daybreak, Jag's sister Shanie was busy sweeping and mopping the wooden floor, with the help of her youngest brother Yog. After this, they prepared a bedroom for the special and highly respected guest who was expected to arrive later in the day. Downstairs in the large kitchen, special foods were being prepared with the help of Nanee (Mama's mother) and Mosee, (Mama's younger sister) and the sweet pungent scent of spices hung thick in the air around the kitchen. It wafted through the open doors and windows to tease the yearning appetite of the large group, who were having a meeting in the bottom-house.

Loaves of bread were bought from the store, and 'dutch-head' cheese was in the process of being grated to prepare a slightly spicy, but delicious cheese spread which was layered on the sliced bread and cut into triangles. The pressure cooker was making its high-pitched, steam-whistling sounds over the hungry flames of the fireside, and the din of pots and pans being washed resounded within the confines of the blue-green painted solid concrete walls of the kitchen. The Mahadeo children always loved when these visits happened, for they were in awe of the personality and character of Dr. Cheddi Jagan, who was the leader of the People's Progressive Party, (PPP) the main and widely popular opposition political party in Guyana.

Dr Cheddi as he was known to everyone, was a man of high moral standing and was idolized in his country for standing up to the dictatorship of the time. He lived his entire life fighting for, and defending the 'small' man. It was an honor for the Mahadeo family to host the great Dr. Cheddi Jagan on his frequent trips to the Lower Corentyne area.

In the little boy's mind, there was the additional benefit of being able to share in the good meals being prepared for Dr Cheddi. He loved the treat of the brown crust from the loaves of bread bought for this occasion, and sharing in the special dishes being prepared. He especially enjoyed the rare, tasty 'dhal-puri' with potato curry and 'kheer' (rice-pudding).

At the 'bottom-house' his father, 'Papa' and elder brother Vishwa, were discussing and planning the security detail which will be necessary throughout the duration of this visit by the highly regarded leader of the opposition party. In this highly influential position, his life was always in danger. On these trips his security detail will involve all the older trustworthy youths from Buddy's gang of boys. They planned in detail, on who will be where and who will be taking what shifts during the nights, standing guard over the entrances to the Village. They also decided on who will be roaming the neighborhood to keep guard from the other directions. This was discussed in great detail and everyone involved were coached on their involvement.

Finally in the evening, around 5 pm, Dr Cheddi Jagan's entourage consisting of five cars approached, and slowly came to a stop on the road. The white Lada carrying the special guest, drove into the yard and parked just inside the gate, while the other four waited by the roadside. The dignified and legendary figure Dr. Cheddi Jagan finally emerged, in awe of those who were gathered to witness his arrival. He greeted everyone in his deep, commanding voice, shook hands all around as a warm, broad smile lit up his otherwise stern face. As was his habit, he paid special attention to the younger ones, with a firm grip of their shoulder, a handshake or a pat on the back. After the greetings, Papa led the way as they went upstairs to show the Doctor to his room, so he could get some well deserved rest.

After a few hours, around dinner time, a truckload of soldiers of the GDF, (Guyana Defense Force) numbering about twenty came to search the house and the people accompanying Dr Cheddi, for illegal weapons. At the time this was normal practice at every one of Dr Cheddi's stops and was a harassment tactic employed by the government on key members of the opposition parties. When the search party filed up the narrow steps, they found the Leader of the PPP sitting upright in the arm-chair. They saluted him and showed him great respect and honor. At their request, Dr Cheddi produced his licensed handgun which he carried for his personal protection. After frisking everyone else who was present in the house, the soldiers seemed satisfied, clambered into the green army truck and roared off.

It was about 9:00 pm, and downstairs at the 'bottom-house' some of Dr Jagan's entourage was finalizing the plan for a series of meetings after a long march with Pandit Mahadeo and his local support group. The guard detail led by Buddy, Vimal, and others, kept the smoke-pot going to help fight off the thick, black swarms of mosquitoes, which prevailed at this time of year because of the wet weather. In the nights, this was the only way that Buddy's group could stay up late outdoor, playing cards and dominoes under the light of the kerosene 'gas' lamp. Old broken, metal cooking pots, which had outlived their usefulness in the kitchen, now served as these smoke pots. The pots were filled with dried coconut shells, and set afire and when they were burning hot and bright, handfuls of green grass were thrown over the dancing flames. This resulted in an almost suffocating, white cloud of smoke which billowed from the pot, and kept the huge swarms of blood-suckers at bay. However, everyone in the immediate area was sure to go to bed smelling somewhat slightly roasted.

Hundreds of people took part in these marches which were being finalized. This one was scheduled for the next day to begin at the town of Skeldon, and the marchers would walk eight miles to Number 63 village, where they will end at the site of a monument dedicated to two young men who were murdered by the soldiers, during a rigged general election a few years ago. In addition to commemorating the anniversary of this event, these marches also showed solidarity with the working masses, and sent a strong message to the dictatorship. During these marches, sometimes the Guyanese soldiers were sent to shadow and show their force, in an effort to scare and intimidate the people who participated.

When Dr Cheddi woke up from his nap later, Papa asked his sons Vishwa (Buddy) and Jag, to give Dr Cheddi's legs a massage. He had already taken part in another march the previous day and his legs were very tired.

The next day was the big day. All the Mahadeo children took part in the march. As Dr. Cheddi led the way, every held up banners and signs, and sang patriotic songs and songs of freedom at the top of their voices as they walked. When the procession filed through each village, the kind inhabitants who could not physically join the marchers came out of their houses and voluntarily gave the marchers snacks, fruits and water, to show their support for the effort. After many long hours, the march finally culminated in a huge gathering of thousands of people at the Number 63 Village monument to the Martyrs, and here they listened intently to Dr

Cheddi Jagan and the rest of the speakers as they delivered their messages of hope and determination, amid cheering and chanting of slogans.

It was a very long and tiring day. After a late dinner, the guest bid his goodbye to his hosts and was driven off to prepare for yet another march the following day.

The tired Mahadeo family finally settled in for a well deserved peaceful night's rest.

Meeting the Swan—Poem

After rollerblading early Sunday morning
I drove to the beautiful beach to sit.
Thought I'd cool down and relish the calm,
Reflect on my life and gather my wit.

There was nary a breeze and not a single wave,
Seems that the ocean was sleeping, snoring in swells.
If this was not the same as heaven,
It surely was the farthest place from hell.

I sat tranquil for a few moments
The rising sun, an awesome sight to see
When I glimpsed, riding the ocean swells,
A white Swan swimming slowly towards me

I held myself still, with bated breath.
And thought I would just let her be.
She stretched her neck and spread her wings
In all her beauty and glory, for me to see

On me her unwavering gaze held
As her large webbed feet hit the wet sand
I admired her pompous royal-like poise
. . . . and her funny, ungainly waddle on land

She shuffled over and sat in the sand,
From me only about three close feet
I looked at her and with my eyes
I said 'my friend it is so good to meet'.

It seemed she understood my
Unspoken language of the eyes

For she looked at me and her eyes said,
'Yes my friend meeting you here is very nice'.

She sat on the beach, and kicked her feet
And threw sand on me as if in play
I felt we were like old friends
Who just ran into each other this day?

She rolled her eyes, flapped her wings and
Sprayed me with water that tasted of salt
I chuckled silently and looked at her.
She was splendid, I could find no fault.

We conversed together, silently as
That moment in time we shared.
Each studying the other
As into each other's eyes we stared.

She was such a graceful creature,
To whom I now felt strangely close.
Deep within me something stirred.
And from me, love and admiration arose.

I wanted to break the silence.
I felt so compelled to speak.
But she softly spoke to me first,
Friendly Swan hisses coming from her beak.

I responded as low and gently as I could.
All I could say was 'hello Swan'.
I felt sad when I realized that
In a few minutes she'll be gone.

She got up and circled around me
Like trying to get a better view
All the while her eyes stayed on me
Like there was something only she knew.

She looked out at the ocean and
I knew it was time for her to go.
She stretched and spread her wings
And wagged her head high and low

I watched her walk to the water
Get in and slowly paddled away.
That surely felt like ten minutes of bliss.
I learnt a lot from Swan that day.

We shared the water and the land on Earth.
And of the same stuff we are both made.
We can live together peacefully with nature.
No need for weapons like a gun or blade.

I learnt there is a common silent language
Among all the creatures of the land
The Swan said that she wished this language
We humans would take the time to understand.

Sunday Morning At The Beach

It was 5:00 AM on Sunday morning, and Mama called on her sons to wake up. This was their Sunday morning routine and Buddy was getting the gang together to go to the beach. Together, they went and called in a loud voice on their uncle's sons Prakash and Satish, their aunt's sons, Vimal and Virjoe, and the rest of the boys who belonged to the group, Somesh, Munesh, Dinesh, Sunny, Goutam, and a few more. The group of about thirteen boys walked down the road towards Number 64 Village and woke the members of the group who lived along the way. Finally, totaling about 20 boys, they headed to the popular # 63 beach.

Here, among the low, rolling sand dunes covered by green snaking vines, they played a game resembling that of cowboys and Indians, which involved a lot of sneaking up and 'killing' the members of the other team. It was a lot of fun for this group of teenage boys, who were a very close-knit group. They did everything together, from playing cricket and volleyball, participating in activities at the Mandir, (Hindu church) and being part of the PPP's youth group, the Progressive Youth Organization (PYO). Unlike the other groups of youths in the neighboring villages, this fun group of teens did not drink, do any drugs, or behave in a rowdy manner. They were very respectable, well behaved, and were true examples of how teenagers should always conduct themselves. Many parents of teenagers in the villages tried to encourage their children to join and 'hang-out' with this group because of the fine example which they set for the community. This group was led by Papa's eldest son Vishwa, and even as a teenager, his commanding presence and strong influence, kept the boys in his gang in line. This inherent leadership quality in his eldest son made Papa very proud, and it showed in his own interaction with the 'gang' when he deferred to Vishwa 'Buddy' to take the lead. His two younger sons, Jag and Yog looked up to their Buddy and tried to emulate him in every way as they grew up.

Their game of 'Indians' came to an end with the brightening sky, as the giant orange orb of the sun peeked up slowly over the horizon, almost like it was rising right out of the ocean. Fingers of intense yellow light split the sky through the distant white clouds, and found the group in formation on the gently sloping beach facing the rising sun. They were being led by Buddy, and slowly duplicated his Yoga exercises in the wet sand, some distance from the breaking waves. Behind them, among the sand dunes in this area of the sea front, a small make-shift hut stood guarding a half-acre of sand, where some brave, prospective soul had planted watermelons. While the relatively tiny vines blended and disappeared into the grass covering the dunes, the green watermelons stood out, dotting the area invitingly as juicy green blobs. Through the tiny opening of what passed for a door, a hammock could be seen with the still-sleeping form of the farmer, who kept watch over his crop against the marauding teenagers, who always tried to sneak a free treat of sweet watermelons, in the darkness of night.

Except for the occasional sound of a slap on skin in response to the few stinging gnats present, or sand-flies as they were commonly known, the only other sound was that of the waves frothing on the surface of the light brown mix of river and ocean waters, fifty feet away.

The scenery was a sobering one of pure and exquisite beauty. Now the huge, golden, rising sun seeming to hover just above the water on the horizon, highlighting a perfectly blue sky through which puffy, cotton-ball clouds floated westwards, at the behest of the swift winds, as if late to some appointed destination. The tall coconut trees about a mile away, danced back and forth to the gusts of wind and beyond them, a farm tractor could be seen pulling a flat open trailer loaded with people, on their way to perform a Sunday morning 'Pooja' at the beach with their family. Multiple flocks of birds flew around, zipping this way and that, as if showing off their superb aerial skills to the funny earth-bound, two-legged creatures below. The peacefulness, strength and aura of this beach, moved most visitors at this time of the morning to a prayerful, peaceful, and contemplative state of mind.

After the group had performed their Yoga exercises, they took part in a game of 'Cocoa' then some playful competition to see who could jump the farthest, run faster, or dig the biggest hole in the sand. Then suddenly, at Buddy's signal, they all made a mad dash to the water, sending the large schools of fish locally known as 'four-eyed fish' (picture) skitting across the surface of the water ahead of the rush of dozens of feet. These fishes looked like they were flying on the surface of the water and moved with great speed, flitting from one wave crest to another effortlessly, before disappearing into the waves.

Now in the water, the boys formed teams and with some climbing onto the shoulders on others, played a game of team wrestling which really was to see who could knock off the other from the shoulder of his rider. This was a lot of fun for the group, and everyone took part in the water games.

As the sparkling sun rose higher in the sky, many smaller groups of people slowly started trickling to the beach, and busied themselves with their Sunday morning prayers and special offerings to their God. Some chose to sit quietly in prayer, but many others performed their ritual of picking water in cupped hands and slowly pouring it in the direction of the blinding sun, while repeating their prayers.

Out in the distance, by the Number 63 Village entrance to the beach, Papa's car, the sky-blue Morris Minor with the license plate PW278 appeared, as Papa slowly drove over the soft, wet sand. He carefully navigated around the stumps of exposed mangrove roots, and clumps of debris and sea grass, which were rejected by the ocean waves. The car's tires left behind two parallel, shiny, water-logged lines in the sand. When they arrived to where the group of youths was frolicking in the water,

Papa, Mama, Nanee and Lil (Shanie) got out and joined the group in the water.

After swimming and playing for another half hour, the boys took to the trail home to get ready for Mandir while Papa, Mama, Nanee and Lil, dried off before climbing into Papa's car for their trip home.

Rivers Of Blood—Poem

The rivers of blood the innocents have shed.
The incessant misery to which they seem wed.
The carnage wreaked at the hands of those who wield power.
Backs against the wall, in terror the poor and weak cower.

Trembling, hiding in fear, and constant pain.
In punishing cold, snow, and freezing rain.
Smoke, smell of gunpowder, and of death.
Any second could be one's last breath.

Burrowing into the ground, like animals they live.
Starving children dying, nothing for fathers and mothers to give.

When will this mindless horror cease?
When will this terrible calamity end?
Why to the unfortunate innocents . . . .
This terror . . . . did God send?

Lunging Alligator

The 'Big-Ben' bicycle wheels skidded, spun and slid, in the low muddy areas with shallow pools of water, and bounced and rattled over the higher, rough, dry spots of dirt, as he pedaled furiously on his way to the rice fields four mile away. The sixteen year old sped over the 'drag-line' bridge, standing on the pedals to avoid the shock of the rough ride from the hard saddle. After bouncing over the hump where the dirt was washed away at the edge of the bridge, he slowed down to check that his 'cutlass' (machete) was still tucked into the slot in the bike frame, just ahead of the rear wheel.

It was just a few months ago when, on a ride over this very bridge, that his machete which he always kept ground to a fine edged blade, had dislodged from its place and caught him on the calf while he was pedaling, slicing a huge inch and a half gash in his lower right leg. He had not realized that his leg was injured, and without stopping, had turned, reset the machete in place, and continued on his journey to the rice field. Only after the three mile ride did he realize that blood from his lower leg was flowing down the pedal to the ground. He had sat down close to the edge of the trail by the waters edge, ripped his shirt into long ribbons, cleaned and bandaged his wound, trying without success to staunch the bleeding. After accomplishing his task of regulating the water level on the rice field he started riding back home. Only then did he discover that he had left a trail of blood dotting the four mile path all the way back to the bridge.

Today, he continued on his way, navigating in and over the muddy ditches made by the tractors, leaving his narrow almost bald, tire tracks in the soft mud. The sky was getting overcast as low, heavy clouds moved in from the south-east. The leading edge of the dark clouds tumbled and rolled over upon itself, as if sneaking up and over the blue skies ahead. The air vibrated with the low rumble of thunder. About a half mile to the east, he could see the sheets of rain falling. It looked like a light gray curtain had suddenly been pulled down by some giant, invisible hand.

He saw a fisherman ahead casting his nets, and started looking around for the discarded live fishes which he had come to expect from these men. Here and there he stopped to throw back the still alive, floundering, unwanted fishes that were left on the bare dirt. As he came across more and more of these stranded fishes, his anger mounted and his face grew a shade darker, as he tried to understand why anyone would do something as cruel as this to other living things.

While he slowly rode by a particularly bad stretch, he saw the fisherman who he thought was responsible for leaving the unwanted fishes on the dry land. The man's 'quake' which was half-full with squirming fishes was propped up in the corner among the weeds. This was a bamboo basket with a thatched cover and a cloth handle in which a fisherman usually kept his catch of fishes.

The fisherman had entered the canal, and was neck deep in the high brown water, struggling to free his net which was apparently stuck in something hidden in the bottom of the muck. The man had not seen him and Jag was still very angry at him for leaving the unwanted fishes to die. He made up his mind that today this man did not deserve any of the fishes because of his heartless behavior, so he dismounted his bike and stealthily crept up to the quake.

Crouching over behind the bushes to remain unseen, he picked up the quake, quickly and quietly walked over to the opposite canal, and emptied the dozen or so fishes into the water by immersing the open quake, then turning it over. He smiled almost in evil glee, as the fishes happily and swiftly shot away, as if overjoyed to once again find freedom. He then replaced the container to the spot from where he had swiped it, mounted his bike, and discreetly rode away, careful to avoid making any bit of noise. When he thought he was far out of the man's earshot, he took off at top speed for the rice fields, skirting carefully through a herd of about thirty cows, being driven by two boys to the savannah, a few miles inland. As he sped down the trail, he surprised many of the common brown lizard usually found in this area. These common, two-foot long creatures were sunning themselves in the open area of the trail, and they skittered away ahead of him, launching themselves into the bushes lining the trail, as he pedaled quickly by.

The air was heavy with the threat of impending rain, and the gray-black clouds seemed to be playing a game of jigsaw puzzle, trying to fill every blue gap in the sky. As they massed together, they proceeded west as if drawing a blanket to hide the blueness still in the western edges of the sky. Jag was in a hurry to get his job completed before it started raining, since riding on the muddy rain-soaked trail was no fun. In those conditions the mud quickly caught and stuck to the wheels and forks of the bicycle, and totally gummed up everything. If that happened he would have to push the bike all the way home.

Bathed in sweat, he finally wheeled to a stop in front their lush green, five acre of rice field, and paused to take a few deep breaths. He then lifted his bike to his shoulder, crossed over the five feet deep side-line trench, and hid the bike in the tall grasses next to the rice field. There he noticed a mass of frothy foam floating in the water among the weeds, which he recognized the nest and eggs of the fish known locally as 'hassa', which was supposed to be a delicacy of the majority fish and meat eating populace.

When a nest like this was found by most people, they 'played' it by putting both hands in the water, and vigorously moving a few fingers back and forth. This intrusion into its hidden nest forced the fish into action, and it was snatched by the waiting hands as it swam between them to defend its eggs. Jag pried and rearranged the tall Para grass to hide the nest from any curious eyes, before grabbing his machete and heading out in the direction of the farm on the 'creek-dam', walking along the 'mare-hee', a narrow earthen berm sprouting tall grasses that separated their flooded field from the neighbor's field.

Today he was not going to do any work on the vegetable farm, but he was hungry and he went there to look for something to eat. He did not have time to make a fire and roast a cassava or an eggplant as he and his Buddy used to do. He finally settled on a large ripe, yellow papaya, which beckoned invitingly in the tree, shaded by the huge ornate leaves balanced at the end of their three feet long, hollow stems. Reaching up on his tippy-toes, he pried the ripe fruit off the tree with his cutlass, and dropped the cutlass just in time to catch the large tender fruit in both hands before it can smash into the ground. Then, like a starving man, whom he surely felt like after his brisk ride, he hurriedly sliced it into four pieces, cleaning the thick fleshy insides free of the little black seeds. While walking back to the rice field, he started eating the delicious, succulent fruit, taking big bites and quickly slurping the juices, as it flowed down his forearm.

The clear water which flooded the field was mostly from the heavy rains over the past week, and was about four to six inches deep. The plants were another four to six inches above the water and a healthy shade of deep green. He enjoyed the sight of the gusts of wind moving the tops of the plants like small gentle rolling waves, in a beautiful sea of emerald green. This was a very tender age for the plants and his main reason for his visit today, was to check for any signs of the dreaded 'heart worm' disease. This infection was in the form of a tiny worm, almost invisible to the naked eye, which attacked and ate the youngest part, or heart of the plant and killed it. If caught in time, he would then have to spray the crop with an insecticide, using the borrowed engine-powered blower from his uncle. If this infection is not caught in time, the entire crop could be decimated in only few days.

He was carrying his machete stuck under his left armpit and held the rest of the papaya in his left hand while eating with his right. His feet made a plunk, plunk, splashing noise, as he walked through the shallow water and the water splashed up playfully around him after each step. He stopped for a few minutes and looking around, saw about four feet ahead what looked like a big toad sitting between the thick rice plants on top of the water. A toad here in this spot seeming to float in the water, certainly looked out of place. Then, about six feet away, he saw the plants swaying back and forth parted by a long, black, pointy tail. He reacted almost in shock, taking a step back as he made out the vague, wide outline of the alligator in the clear water, where it pressed down the tender rice plants. At the same moment that his brain galvanized him into action, the alligator's did also, whipping its tail around as it lunged towards him, it's huge jaws agape, displaying a fearsome array of sharp protruding teeth in the pink cavernous mouth. Jag dropped his pieces of papaya, grabbed his machete from under his left arm, and swung wildly as the reptile closed in on him. He kept moving to the side and chopped as hard as he could, aiming anywhere at the body of the alligator which he could reach. His sharp machete made dull metallic, thudding sounds on the hard, scaly skin of the alligator, and he kept swinging the blade almost in pure panic. A few of his strikes caught the creature on the side of it's eyes and head, and even when it stopped moving forward, the boy, propelled by his intense fear, kept slashing away at the black beast. After what seems like hundreds of strikes with his broad, heavy steel blade, he finally realized that the alligator was no longer moving towards him, but it stood in place, head raised, shaking and quivering in the throes of death. The boy stood heaving, gulping in great gasps of breaths, watching as life seemed to very slowly exit the contorting body of this magnificent beast, and its giant head slowly settled into the now pink-splotched water.

As realization sunk in, he slowly walked over on trembling knees to the 'mare-hee'. Here he sat down shaking with overwhelming fear and the rush of adrenaline still flowing through his body. A good ten minutes later, he crept back slowly and quietly, and after making sure that the beast was really dead, grabbed and pulled it by the rough, jagged tail to the 'side-line' dam about a hundred feet away, leaving a temporary flattened path, through the flexible plants.

For some reason he could not explain at the moment, he was now filled with sadness and deep remorse. Even though he was forced to defend himself, he felt really guilty about killing the alligator. Why did the creature have to die at his hands? What if he had taken another path through the field, or did not come to the backdam today, then the beautiful creature would still be alive? This incident bothered him for days and he could not stop thinking about it. Finally he settled on what his parents taught him about karma and its consequences, and in his mind he used this as justifications for his actions.

This Cruel Life—Poem

I have never been one of much wealth.
I've tried hard to take care of my health.
Lived my life mostly by the book!
Stayed within the limits . . . . whatever it took!

To some of my problems I had an answer,
Then my doctor told me I had breast cancer.
I had always waited for my luck to run hot.
Now I feel . . . . like I've just been shot.

Oh, how cruel this life can be!
Why is this happening to me?

My share of mistakes . . . . I have done.
Fears of facing them . . . . I had none.
But this all crept up on me with stealth.
How can I play this hand that I've been dealt?

Now I know not what to do.
Am I dreaming? Or is this all true?
How much more of this, can I take,
Before my strong spirit it does bend and break?

I have always been one of confident strength,
And bold personality . . . . wherever I went!
Always held my head up with pride.
Nothing I ever felt I needed to hide.

Now I undergo bouts of radiation and chemo
My stomach is sick and my energy level low
All the pain and frequent trips to the doctor

But I hide it all so well as any good actor

My skin is changing colors and I'm really pale
My joints and bones ache so and my eyes fail
My beautiful long hair is falling out in clumps
And on my once smooth skin, now little weird bumps

But I will not give up, not without a fight!
Use all my willpower and all my might!
Useless tears of frailty I shall not shed!
I shall not give up and just lay in my bed!

Signs of weakness I will resist and not show,
It is something that I have never known.
Now, what can I do? What can I say?
Except to hold my head up high and pray.

Life . . . What Is It?—Poem

(Share a laugh with me)

If life was a game, I would ensure I come out on top.
If it was a battle I would try my best to win.
Was life an examination? I would study very hard.
If it was a glass with drink, mine would be filled to the brim.

If life was a worthy book, I would read it to the last page.
Was it great music, to mine everyone would dance.
If life was the hands of a clock, I would slow it down,
And if it was a gamble, I would take every single chance.

If life was a painting, my hands would be as steady as a rock.
Was it someone else's dream, I would make sure it's not a nightmare.
If life was a table of food mine would be gourmet.
And if it was a horror movie, everyone . . . . I would scare.

If life was a prayer, I would make myself a saint.
If it was a spaceship, I would take mine to the most distant star.
If life was the wind I would be gentle and soothing
If it was a beam of light mine would pierce the darkness, way afar.

But if life was all Love and Romance,
I would be the world's biggest Romeo.

The Papaya Medicine Tree

Directly across the road, lived one of Papa's sisters whom they all called Phuwa (meaning Father's sister). Vimal was Phuwa's elder son, and his siblings were Indira, Amrita, and Virjanand. Vimal was so close to Papa and Buddy that he was almost a part of the immediate family. He was a fun and daring person and was always with Buddy and willing to help whenever asked.

A few years ago they used to live on the western back street, almost directly behind Papa's own yard, in a little house which was off the ground on stilts. Since then, they had moved that little house on a truck, and combining it with their Aja's (father's father) house, lived in the house together with their grandfather and grandmother. It was a convenient location for them since Vimal's father was a carpenter and quite the handyman. He came over often to help fix windows and cupboards whenever there was the need at Jag's home.

Vimal's Aja, was a very kind old man who came over almost every day to chat with Mama, and always had fun pointing out the funny pictures in the daily newspapers. Every so often he brought over strange and different vegetable plants and roots, which he would plant in Mama's garden. He spent most of his days at the rice fields, and at his farm, and was always seen with his shovel or machete in hand.

His wife Ajee, as all the children called her, had a few medical issues including diabetes. She was a very nice old lady who walked very slowly and spoke sparingly. Next to the kitchen drain in Papa's yard, there grew a ten feet tall papaya tree which helped to shade the corner of the yard with it wide umbrella of giant ornate, green leaves, each supported by a half inch thick, hollow, tube-like stem.

This tree was always loaded with dozens of green papayas, which were never allowed to ripen because Agee used one green fruit every day to treat her illness. She spoke softly in broken English and every morning she came over, took the stick with the little hook which was kept standing in the corner of the house, reached up and pulled down one green papaya.

She then carried the green fruit home, with its stem dripping a white milky liquid as if crying after being separated from its parent tree. There she threw together her secret concoction which she consumed each day. But over many years she still grew frail and sicklier as time dragged on.

This routine went on for many years, and then the strangest of things happened. One morning it was discovered that Ajee had passed away quietly in her sleep, sometime during the night. The news came as dawn was breaking. After Papa's family had gathered across the street for a while with his sister's family, Mama headed to the kitchen to prepare breakfast for her family. Upon opening the solid wooden kitchen window that looked out upon the trunk of the papaya tree she discovered that the medicine papaya tree which Ajee depended on for so many years had fallen down during the night. It was as if the tree refused to keep living, when the old lady who depended on it daily, had died. This also came as quite a shock since when most papaya trees fell over, either blown over by winds or heavy rains, the few roots still in the ground usually kept the tree fully alive and still productive. But this particular tree fell over and somehow had been completely uprooted and now lay on its side, dead.

And as if in defiance, in a desperate, last ditch attempt to give freely of its green medicine fruits, the dozens of green, oblong fruits were flung all over the immediate area, leaving splotches of white milky stains upon the dry earth.

Religion! God's Way?—Poem

Of all God's creations in this world,
I could never understand,
Why so much dislike and distrust,
Between the religions in all the land.

The teachings of all the religions,
Is supposed to be for the good of man.
But sometimes it seems that none of this,
ever go according to the divine plan.

Of his many names not one is wrong
Over this in God's name, they kill
Can't we accept, He is but one?
And killing is against the one God's will?

God never needs His many Names
to be defended by you or me.
He is much more powerful than that,
Can't we open our eyes and see?

People, entombed alive, and killed,
to try and force them to convert.
Is that what their religion taught them?
That in God's name, it's okay to kill and hurt.

Who said that to convert Religion?
from one to the other is the best.
Do you always drive the same road to town?
When you approach from the east or west?

Why do we fail to understand?

All religions are but a different road,
To that one place we all vie for,
The one and only heavenly abode.

To kill in the name of God,
Is it not rather wrong and unfair?
Destroying something which belongs
to one you say you love and hold dear.

And the belief of some people,
after killing, to add injury to insult.
they go in their church to pray,
never realizing what their prayers are worth.

Even in this modern day and age,
wars we are fighting, wars we will start.
To think our religion is better than others
Cause entire countries to be torn apart.

Do we have to follow religion?
Is which God do we believe?
Why are we given a choice anyway?
When by nature's simple rules, we could all live.

When will we all truly realize?
When will all of us finally awake?
To think that God is partial to any Religion,
is such a terribly big mistake.

When will ordinary people wake up?
When will we all see the light?
God never wanted us to be religious fanatics,
God never wanted any of us to fight.

No 68 Primary School

(Late 1960's to early 1970's)

At first glance it seemed that No. 68 Primary School was flung into the only open space available in the area, about a quarter mile west of the main road at the middle of No. 68 Village. The three streets that intersected as a T shape immediately in front of the school yard were topped with red bricks which were strewn about leaving a rough, bumpy, street surface.

These commonly used bricks were created by burning clay in huge bonfires. The exposed edges of these bricks which were once jagged and sharp were eventually tamed and worn smooth by the hundreds of innocent, bare little feet that lovingly caressed them each and every school day. A few hundred feet to the north and to the south, the ten to fifteen feet wide streets deteriorated to mere dirt trails, pockmarked by large mud holes. These were first initiated by the farm tractors driving by in the wet season, and then perfected into round play mud-holes by the pigs, which Mr. Peter allowed to roam around the area.

The primary school was a two story high wooden structure with wide corridors to the north, framed by banister railings about four feet high. The floor was polished smooth by the same hundreds of bare little feet which had conquered the sharp red bricks out on the streets. These corridors which overflowed with energetic, screaming children at each break, curled around at both ends into wide staircases which connected both floors. The lower floor held what was called at the time, the Prep A, Prep B, 1st Standard and 2nd Standard classrooms. The second floor housed the 3rd, 4th Standard, 1st form and 2nd form. (Names of grades at the time) The school dress code was a standard uniform. The girls' uniform comprised of a white top and maroon/burgundy skirt and the boys wore light blue shirts and khaki short pants. Since most families at the time could not afford shoes or even simple slippers, almost everyone went to school barefooted except for the teachers.

Teachers at this school still administered corporal punishment by hand, with a ruler or a cane, by striking the buttocks or the hands of the guilty student for misbehavior or simply for missing homework. Mr. M who taught 4th standard was known to be particularly tough on his students. There were quite a few instances when a few parents of students who objected to the punishment administered by this teacher, visited the school fighting mad, and actually got into physical confrontations with him. As expected, these incidents always created quite a stir among the students with the young ones naturally choosing sides based on the punished student, and their like or dislike of Mr. M. Mr. Dripaul who taught Jag's and his sister Shanie's classes was easier and more effective as a teacher since he was more patient, diplomatic, and lenient with his students.

Back in 1969-1970, the fenced in yard of the school bordered some interesting neighbors. On the left was Walter Peters who reared dozens of pigs, and slaughtered them for sale to the meat markets. Sometimes during classes, the loud mournful squealing could be heard from the pigs meeting their tortuous demise. Mr. Peters wielded his will of death, by forcing the helpless animals into a corral-like structure which was just wide enough for the body of the creature. Then tying it securely in place, he straddled the animal facing it's head, held it's pointy head up, and swung a heavy metal hammer with his muscular right arm, aiming at the wide spot right between the rolling eyes, which mirrored pure fear. As the animal screamed, and contorted itself against the restraining ropes in agony, he continued to swing mercilessly until the creature finally slumped over, twitching in defeat and eventual death. Then he tasked himself with hanging the heavy carcass up by its hind legs in the hot tropical sun, and surrounded by swarms of black flies, he skinned and hacked it into the desired pieces, which his customers had requested.

Directly across the street was a little shack, which was accessed by crossing over a rotting, four foot bridge of wooden planks built over the drainage ditch. This decrepit shack was owned and run by Mrs. Punia. Her cabinets and shelves displayed the temptations of sweet treats such as sugar-cake, something called long-sweetie, stretchers, gataa, and tamarind balls. She also made and sold home made drinks, and here the more fortunate children spent their ten to twenty five cents daily allowance. Competing for her easily influenced, young customers, was a larger establishment directly across the main entrance to the school, known

175

as Bony's. This was a ten times bigger version of its smaller competitor, with a longer, wider bridge, and sold a bigger variety of delicacies such as pastries and bottled colas. It featured benches on two of its four sides, which encouraged the young customers to sit around and spend their money. It also gave an excellent vantage point from where to view the sporting events, which took place on the play field across the way. Many other vendors sat by the school gates under umbrellas and also vied for the attention of the same customers. They sold treats such as cubes of milky, sugary ice called 'ice-blocks', crude popsicles, spicy, hard-fried chick peas, and curried green mangoes.

The playground was actually a borderless cricket ground, where the school held its outdoors student assemblies on beautiful sunny days. It was also where the school sporting activities such as racing and softball games took place. The annual and popular school sports-day was also done here. This day was when the students participated in team sports and fun events against each other. It was during one of these event days, when Jag and his sister Shanie had found almost ten dollars in bills and change, while walking the one mile to school early in that morning. The money was laying flat in the dirt next to the new Lions Club sign, directly across his Chacha's house at No. 66 Village. At the time, ten dollars was an awful lot of money, and even though they both tried very hard, they could not spend it all on that day of sports at the school.

To the west of the cricket ground was almost a semi-marshy wasteland. This was where the more adventurous children gathered to catch a glimpse of a family of alligators that made this patch of wet wilderness, their home. Small groups of brave students usually gathered here, attempting to mimic the 'ugh, ugh, ugh' of the baby alligator, to try and tease the big mother alligator out of hiding. Whenever she did show herself, it was much to the delight of the children, and there was much celebratory whooping from the boys and 'oohs' and 'aahs' from the girls.

Behind Mrs. Punia's shop was Sharma's rice mill, which was ringed by unkempt trees and bushes. The tallest of these was a forty to fifty feet tall tree, which flowered and bore a beautiful winged seed. On a windy day, these two inch winged seeds fluttered, spun and danced all around and blew into the school in little colorful clouds, much to the enjoyment of the children. This rice mill also billowed small white puffs of steam and its diesel engine hummed constantly. To those truly in the mode of teaching or learning however, these noises, including that of the squealing pigs nearby, slowly dissipated and eventually disappeared into daily non-existence. After 4th Standard class at this school, the students usually took the Common Entrance Examinations which, when passed, allowed them to enter into High School.

At the back of Bony's shop, was the place that most of the boys considered to be the most fun place at school. Here in the damp red sand with short grass and scrubby undergrowth, a few huge mango trees rose out of the earth, with rough twisting trunks about three feet thick. In the abundant branches of these trees, many of the boys took turns playing the popular 'shy-goolie' game with their friends. In this game, as the school break bell sounded, the last boy on a mad dash to the tree will have to be the catcher. One of the first took a stick, and from under his legs flung the stick as far away as he possible could. While the catcher runs to retrieve the stick, the rest of the group clambered into the tree as far out of reach of the catcher as they could. These trees had numerous strong, big branches covered by large, dark green leaves. The size of these trees made this kind of game quite a daunting challenge for the catcher. After retrieving the thrown stick, he has to leave the stick at the base of the tree, climb up and try to catch one of the boys already safely in the tree, while making sure that no one sneaked down and took the stick. If this happens, then he has to start all over again. However, if he protects his stick, and catches someone then that person becomes the 'catcher'.

Jag attended this school from 1965 to 1971 and during the first four years, he was accompanied by his older sister Shanie. They left home together each morning and took turns carrying the lunch pail they called the 'saucepan'. At lunch the two walked another half mile from the school to their Nanee's (grandmother) home a village away at No. 69 Village. Here they entered through the back gate and made their way through the big vegetable garden and tall swaying coconut trees, to the house by the main road. Their Nanee usually found some fruits to supplement the lunch from their lunch pail, and their Nana (grandfather) always seemed to find some rare fruit such as sapodillas for them to enjoy. He was a quiet old man who rarely spoke, but always tried to do kind things with his grandchildren.

His ways of showing kindness were unique. When he found a soursop which is ready to be picked, he sent a message with one of their cousins, Prabha, Shobha, or Rambha to tell Jag or Shanie to go there for lunch, so that he can take the two to the tree and have them pick the ripe fruit off the tree themselves.

After his sister passed the Entrance Examinations and started going to Line Path Secondary School, Jag walked to school alone. In a few weeks however, he became friends with Giresh who was his neighbor's son and was the same age as himself. For reasons the boys could not understand to this day, Giresh's parents did not want the two to be friends. Because of this, even though the two lived next door to each other, they left home separately and whoever reached the creek bridge first, waited for the other, before continuing the walk to school together. The school was to the south, almost exactly a mile away from home, and they walked through the back streets of Number 67 Village to get there. On the way, they passed by the Goobie tree (Calabash) which was in front of Bahie's (pronounced as in Baw-ee) rice mill. This was where Jag would usually double over in pain at least a few times a week. He loved sugar roti but when he eats a lot of sweet, about twenty minutes later his stomach would hurt for a few minutes. This calabash tree marked where the twenty minutes would be reached almost every day. He never told his parents because he did not want to stop eating his sugar-roti. Then the two walked past the middle-walk canal where many boys from the school would skip classes after lunch, to go swimming and to play in the murky waters. From here, they walked past a street in the back of the village on which there were no houses. The western side of this dirt street was thickly wooded. In these woods just before the Eeto (pronounced as in eight-o) rice mill, there grew a unique plant known as the 'leaf-of-life'. (picture) The succulent leaves of this plant had a jagged edge from where, under the right environment, roots and little plants sprung.

To the amazement and delight of many of the little children, one of these perfect environments just happened to be between the pages of a school text book. Many of them stopped in these woods on the way home from school, to pick these leaves and place them in each of their books, where after a week the leaves sprouted many roots along the edges. This plant also had numerous medicinal properties and is used in many tropical areas around the world.

This was the school life of children in the late 1960's and early 1970's. Almost all children walked to school bare-footed, studied by the light of kerosene hand lamps, and played with self-made toys, yet it was by all accounts, happy times and a happy life.

Against My Better Judgment—Poem

I did not listen to my own intuition,
Now I'm trapped in the world of cravings.
I never acted as my conscience told,
Now I wallow in the pain my obsessions bring.

I let my guard down only once
Awoke feeling trapped in quicksand.
Could not move, could not think
Then again turn to my addiction for a hand.

I lay down on my bed . . . . half asleep,
gnash my teeth, toss and turn
And deep, deep within my being
The desire for more . . . burn and burn.

I wake up suddenly in a cold-sweat
With my heart pounding and racing.
Sanity, I tried and cannot keep
With my mind's frantic pacing.

I cannot eat . . . . my appetite's shot.
God! What I would do for a hit.
From my own mother I would steal.
My own lover's throat I would slit.

My body tremble, my hands shake.
I feel so totally out of control.
For some relief, even to the Devil
I would certainly sell my very soul.

I tried to pass the blame to my friends.

Denied my pain was of my own making.
All the while slipping deeper and deeper,
Refusing any help, free for the taking.

Of my innocence, I've convinced myself.
And justified everything which I've done.
Enduring endless hours of insanity,
For just a few painful hours of fun.

Over this precipice I should not have gone
I should not have taken that very first step.
I should have listened to my own intuition.
Then my devil and his demons, I would not have met.

Confusion's End—Poem

Please tell me why I cannot think,
why I cannot sleep another wink.
All my thoughts, all of them muddled,
with all of this, I grow increasingly puzzled.

I cannot figure out any of it,
Nothing I can think of helps, not one bit.
I try to sort them out one by one,
but in a flash, even the effort is gone,

Into the raging tempest of my mind
Please, I'll try anything to unwind.
I tried to drown these thoughts with drink,
But the little devils swim better than I think.

I drift in and out of tortuous, fitful sleep
Only to wake up so many times and weep,
For now the fighting so deep inside
has opened my painful wounds, oh so wide.

I can't fully express this way I feel
My mind's in a daze and does not seem real
My broken thoughts I try hard to mend,
I even thought of putting it all to an end.

Then one early morning, in a daze,
I rode to the ocean beach, I was amazed.
I stood in the sand for while in contemplation,
And tried to make sense of my situation.

I sat on the sand and closed my eyes.

I thought I fell asleep, it felt so nice.
It felt as though all my torture and pains,
were being washed away in heavenly rains.

My eyes opened to the dawning light,
As yet, not another single soul in sight.
Ever so slowly, to my sad eyes
came the realized beauty of the sunrise.

A deep breath drawn of the fresh morning air
and now everywhere around me, all I can hear,
The magnificence of nature coming alive
sweet sounds to my ears and before my eyes.

The waves and the birds loudly calling
As if in their unique way 'good morning'
Hold on! Wait a minute! I feel okay!
I can now think straight on this new day!

A prayer I knew flowed through my head
My life-force returned, I now felt undead
I can now, clear and with much more ease,
sort my mangled thoughts out, piece by piece.

Now I feel alive, so much in control,
I was suddenly joyous in my new role.
I feel now like the Master of my mind!
The slave in me, now I will leave behind!

I enjoy this precious moment and realize,
maybe Nature and God have made me wise.
Could it be that God and Nature are the same,
in all of His amazing creation except in name?

With this eternal question in my head,
I realized slowly that I'd rather be dead.
Than to feel as confused as I have been,
with this revelation that I have now seen.

I lifted my head up to the sky and slowly pray,
Thank you Lord, I know not what to say,
I'm so sorry that I was blind and did not see
All of this peace that you've made for me.

Now that I have realized and seen all of this
Your creation and shadows of the eternal bliss,
I pray and promise you, I'll try my best
I'll walk that line and I'll pass your test.

The Dark Side of Me—Poem

I feel like the dark devil is riding me,
So blinded with rage and fury I cannot see.
Cannot be intimidated I have no fear.
To choose right or wrong I do not care.

Every single day with every breath
face to face I spit in the eye of death.
The raging monster in me wants to kill
don't care who it is, be dead by my will.

I have to hurt, punish and maim,
sorrow, tears and blood, it shall rain.
Let love go to hell, all I want is hate
Hell's my playground, with the devil I have a date.

Frustrations in me builds, deep and high,
desire to crush and destroy, no reasons why.
I care not who suffers, friend or foe.
I do not give a damned I don't want to know.

I'll laugh in your face and watch you die
stomp on your grave with fire in my eye.
So when you're ready step into my realm
You will pay either way and forever be damned.

Waywardly Meandering-My Mind—Poem

Intensely loud, ceaseless-silent rumble
Across wide open boundless space
Immeasurable and effortless energy
Rolling through . . . . unique, shapeless grace.

Waywardly meandering unexplored
Uncharted, depth-less . . . . yet familiar caverns.
Immense forward momentum through
All unbreakable barriers under the sun.

Pierced through and through by formless
Tethering tentacles of life-forms.
Repository for nefarious residues of
Inanimate, animate, moribund and dead.

The nucleus of perpetual motion-
Time almost unknown, non-existent,
Thundering through tenebrous hellish canyons
Into luminously-brilliant heavenly expanses.

Roaring silently-inaudible murmurs into
Undiscovered rooms of tranquility and solitude
. . . . then into loud incessant hubbub
-sea of unrestrained pandemonium.

Quaking, pulsating-uncontrollable,
unpredictable . . . . physically lusting
angrily endeavoring to encompass
all within and even beyond reach.

Continuously flowing eternal power
Never-ceasing . . . . non-ending
Ravenously absorbing, swallowing all exposed
With putrid stench and sweet fragrances.

Concealing immense troves of treasure
Never and forever un-revealed
Unrealized efficient solutions
Amid on-going extremes of tortuous confusion.

Never harnessed, near impossible to control
Unfathomable extreme contrast in characters
Unavoidable . . . . yet elusive, unequaled potency
Never-ending, forever,
uncontrollably flowing . . . . MY MIND.

Dew Drops—Poem

Did you ever wake up just before dawn,
to admire the beauty of the beaming sunrise?
To gaze at that glowing orb, low on the horizon,
With it's blazing light-shafts and awesome size?

Instead of cursing the birds outside your window,
Did you ever make the effort and go out?
To share in their part of nature's splendor,
And hear melodious singing from beaked mouths?

Have you ever taken the time to appreciate
the morning frenzy of the little bees?
Or observed the array of colorful birds
feeding their young, in and among the trees?

Have you ever left your damp foot-prints
trailing in the green, dew-covered grass?
Or kissed a few cool dewdrops off a leaf
As you slowly, tenderly brush past?

Have you ever gone outside in the light rain
in a quiet, peaceful and lonely place?
And looked up to the heavens just to
feel the refreshing drizzle on your face?

Have you ever gazed up in wonderment and awe
At the cotton-ball clouds way up high?
And wonder, what exactly is way beyond
all that wide expanse of deep blue sky?

When last have you gone to the park,
and in the woods, stopped and sniffed?
The fragrance of the grass, trees, and flowers,
where so many of God's creatures live?

Have you ever gone to the beautiful beach
Way before anyone else got there?
And enjoyed watching the seagulls feeding
and smelled the saltwater in the air?

Or have you ever seen the huge sun at dusk
while sitting quiet and peaceful at that beach?
When the blazing setting sun seemed to be
so close, like within a long stick's reach?

Did you ever walk outside into the dark night
minutes before you go to sleep?
And marveled at the moon and stars,
as into your being, true tranquility seep?

These questions I bring to you today
That hopefully they will help you find.
A glimmer of happiness if you have none,
or a little deep harmony of some kind.

As we get closer to God or Nature,
We will slowly, but surely realize
That by pausing to enjoy these moments
Some peace of mind will slowly arise.

A Tribute 'Mama'—Poem

I remember myself as a little boy,
making a small match-box toy.
So mischief and sometimes very rude,
But at meal-time My Mama would say,
"come on my son, eat your food."

I remember the day my first dog died
and how I sat down and cried and cried.
Then I took him out back . . . . by the drain,
and buried him there while it rained.
My Mama cuddled me . . . . her eyes bright.
"Don't worry Jag, everything will be alright."

The first litter of kittens from our black cat.
Cute little creatures, pudgy and fat.
Tortured them roughly in play,
. . . . my mother would see.
"Jag, would you please leave them be?"

Tease my little brother . . . . make him cry.
It was just fun, I don't know why.
Knocked him over, standing on a chair,
he fell screaming with blood in tears.
Mama came running out of the house
the anger in her was now aroused.
Attending to my brother's bleeding head,
"You are such a bad boy!" to me she said.

I would steal and create havoc,
scream and fight and run amuck.
When in trouble for my deviltry,

I'd hide with my books in my tamarind tree.
Even so bad, but when it's time to eat
Mama would say "come down
. . . . you, no one would beat."

Papa asked my big brother one time
"check the car fluids, make sure all is fine."
I dropped the car's hood on his head,
his head bleeding, I thought he was dead.
Mama came out . . . . she was so mad.
"My God, why do you have to be so bad?"

A devil I was . . . . our house I set afire
with a pile of papers and an old car tire.
If the fire our neighbor did not see,
Don't know what would have become of me!
The fire put out, the neighbor thanked,
and well deserved . . . . my bottom was spanked.

The new car seats, I cut up with a razorblade
to see why it's soft and of what it's made.
The sofa cushions, I would tear
and pull the insides out . . . . made them bare.
My sister's piggy-bank . . . . I would raid,
and start trouble by pulling on her braids.

I was like a big painful blister,
fighting with my little brother and sister.
My sister I would tease and joke
and my little brother, I'd fight and choke.
Over all this Mama would yell.
I remember putting her through all this hell.

Well deserved punishment for things I did,
after a while Dear Mama would forgive.
I did so much to make her sad,
. . . . but she'd still say
"You're my Devta . . . just a little bad."

191

All of us around the table at night,
doing our homework by
. . . . kerosene-lamp-light.
I would sneak and read my comic book
whenever Mama was busy and did not look.
Mama would say "Son you'd better study,
so you don't have to work the rice fields
. . . . and get all muddy."

I was always hobbling with bruises and cuts,
and bumps from falling while
. . . . doing something nuts.
Recuperating under my Mama's studious care,
me without an injury . . . . was very rare.
Hurt falling off bicycles
. . . . and nasty dog bites.
Come home from school
. . . . bloodied from fights.
Through all this my Mama would hide
Much of my naughtiness from my Papa's sight.
There was a time or two when I cut school,
back then I was such a gullible little fool.
Things I would do, the games I would play,
Some, no one else knows of . . . . till this day.
Most of the time I was a little terror,
A little kid . . . . couldn't separate the errors.
But overall, I was a very happy child.
Just overly curious, and a bit half-wild.

In hindsight, without Mama's guiding hand,
Which, to my life, was a glorious magic wand.
But I learnt to tell between wrong and right
and as I grew up, I finally saw the light.

Now, when these memories come to mind,
I see my Mama's face, loving and kind.
Down deep in my heart I now realize,

It is she who has made me wise.
And what I have now grown up to be,
I hope is what she had envisioned of me.

Little devil I was, but you taught me love.
You taught me to pray to the great one above.
So many, your lessons, I will never forget,
your patience to reach the standards we set.

I will always do to make you proud
The things to set me apart from the crowd.
You are by far, the best Mother on Earth,
I thank God that you were chosen . . . . for my birth.

I Love You Ma.
Your Son Jag.

Shafts Of Light—Poem

Sitting upon the beach in the early dawn,
with my peaceful surroundings, I became one.
From out of nowhere came the urge
to try and make me and nature merge.

I try to be very quiet, sit with bated breath,
and hold very, very still . . . . as still as death.
I listen carefully, ever so slightly I can hear,
like whispered words, floating about in the air.

I stay motionless, make like a stone,
I can even hear the earth grumble and moan.
I take in the sweet, rugged music of the waves,
its very low roaring, like an echo in a cave.

From far away, out over the horizon
came the first glorious rays of the sun.
The bright edge of the blazing, fiery disk,
cut right through the low hanging morning mist.

This awesome and wondrous sight made me smile,
As I enjoyed this dawn magic for little awhile.
The clouds that were moments ago so puffy white,
being parted by beaming shafts of yellow light.

Shades of orange yellow, crimson and red,
Tranquility now slowly seeps into my head.
Then into the waves fell one bright beam,
shattered into a million pieces . . . or so it seem.

Like bits of diamond mixed into the froth,

into the churning waves that the ocean wrought.
All of a sudden, the air filled with sweet sound,
of all God's creatures waking up all around.

The birds from the trees all took to the air,
with such a whoosh, so sweet to my ear.
Even the gulls started doing their splendid dance,
swooping this way then that, like in a trance.

Little creatures all around me stirring,
all ready to welcome in the new morning.
I feel so insignificant, I feel so small,
I am in awe, in wonderment of it all.

I could not help but slowly smile as I think,
I would not miss this to sleep another wink.
Everyone else at home, asleep in their beds,
all their tensions still tight inside their heads.

When nature's therapy is here, free for all,
But many pretend ignorance, don't heed the call.
Whatever today prompted me to do this?
I am thankful to be here and experience this bliss.

Never may figure out the reason for my birth.
But I am grateful to be put here on Planet Earth.

Thank You Dear God

Misery—Poem

When I have lost the spring in my step,
And by my own strength, my basic needs cannot be met.

When a smile is no longer on my face,
When I cannot move, bedridden, and in one place.

When to those I love pain and sorrow is all I bring,
and about the misery in their lives . . . . I can do nothing.

When I cannot speak that which I ache to say
and my loved ones cannot bear to see me like this everyday.

When my body-sick, useless and ravaged by time
and my senses have no control, like they are no longer mine.

I hope and I pray, and please, don't ask me why.
Pull the plug . . . . Release me and just let me die.

About the Author

I was born on 11th August 1962 to Budhram Mahadeo 'Papa' and Rajkumaree Mahadeo 'Mama' and given the name Jagdeep. I am the fourth of five children. My siblings are Vidya 'Deedee', Vishwa 'Buddy' or 'Bhaiya', Vishwanie 'Shan' or 'Lil' and Yoganand 'Yog'.

I attended No. 68 Primary School and after passing the Common Entrance Examination, was accepted into Tagore Memorial High School in 1973. The five years of high school flew by and most of the stories told in this book occurred during those impressionable years. My 'addiction' at the time was comic books ranging from the 'Commando' series, to 'Superman' and 'Ironman' series, and my obsession in reading these comics negatively impacted my schoolwork. After completing Forms 1 through 4, (Guyana having the British Education System this is equivalent to US 8 through 11 Grade) I kicked my studies into high gear only in Form 5, a few months before the final GCE 'O' level examinations (General Certificate of Education is an academic qualification boards in the United Kingdom)

This was when I finally realized how serious my education was and how it will influence the rest of my life, and this too was only after many discussions with Mama, my elder sister Vidya, and my Mamoo. (Mother's brother) When Mama saw that I was finally serious about my studies, she volunteered to wake me up at 3:00 am each school day so that I could study in the relative peace and quiet of the morning. This approach worked and I passed all seven subjects of the GCE which I took in 1978.

The following year was spent planting rice, tending the vegetable gardens and holding a part-time carpenter's job (learning carpentry) with my Mosa (the husband of my mother's sister) from No. 47 Village which was about eight miles away. During this time, I rode my bicycle the eight miles in the morning to work at the construction job at No. 48 Village and back home in the afternoon. On days when my bike was in disrepair, I paid for a ride on the Tata bus. During the weekends, I also performed religious services for families as my brothers also did. These ceremonies were arranged by Papa and sometimes were seven consecutive nights of 'Havan' services.

A few months later, at the insistence of my sister Vidya, I took the entrance exam to attend the Guysuco technical training school in Port Mourant. This highly respected school—the Port Mourant Training Centre—developed young minds into the technicians, mechanics, electricians, machinists and engineers which the sugar industry, and most other industries needed. I entered the Training Center as part of class of 1979 and spent the next two years living on campus and studying as a Fitter Machinist (Machinist/Engineer). This four year course was designed so that the first two years were spent in the college, and the last two years working as an apprentice at the machine shop at the Skeldon Sugar Factory.

After finishing the four year course and graduating in 1983, I worked at the sugar factory over the next few years as a machinist and shift mechanic in both, the night and day shift.

I met my wife, Dee and we were married in 1984. On 20ᵗʰ July 1985, I left Guyana for New York City in the United States. Since I came from a fairly quiet village, I was used to the country life and I found the size, hustle and bustle, and loudness of New York City to be somewhat uncomfortable. I worked at a Machine Company which was located on the fourth floor of a building on Canal Street in Manhattan. The work was prototype machining and this job helped me to hone my conventional machining skills and take it to the next level, but I kept hearing about CNC machining (Computerized Numerical Controlled) from my co-workers and was curious to learn. In 1987, my discomfort in NYC and my yearning to learn more led me to Long Island where I landed a job to work and learn CNC machining at a machine shop located in Hauppauge. The opportunity at here allowed me to learn and apply my newfound engineering and machining skills, and here the kind owner gave me, a willing worker, the keys to the Machine shop and fourteen hour workdays. This expanded my opportunity so that in May of 1988 we bought our first home at 35 Tamarack Street in Central Islip.

Six months later our first blessing came in the form of our son Avinash, the cutest little baby boy who was born on the 18ᵗʰ of January 1989. The second blessing came as our beautiful little darling daughter Vashti Devi, who was born on the 4th of December 1992 and this started a journey of happiness which continues to this day.

In November 1989, the company closed its doors but not before the owner found employment for myself and his other employees. I was sent to work at another Machine Company in Lindenhurst and my fortunes multiplied. The owner, Ron, was a kind hearted man in every way imaginable and had immense patience with his employees. His wife Liz worked in the office and alone, she fulfilled all the duties required in a business office. The years at this company was spent honing my mechanical and engineering skill-set and this is where I befriended another unique individual, Neil. He was the Quality Manager and over the years, he taught me the tricks of inspection, helped when anyone grew frustrated over the stresses of the job, and kept the environment in which we worked encouraging and light-hearted. In the next few years he would suffer many major setbacks to his health but his demeanor, mental strength and spirit never faltered. Here was someone from whom I learned and continue to learn the lessons of mental strength and courage. We are still friends to this day. My family is still honored to have him and his sweet wife Brenda come over to our home for the occasional dinner where we sit and enjoy Dee's vegetarian cooking.

After 13 years at this machine shop, new opportunities for advancement knocked and I took the position of Lead at a Machine shop in Ronkonkoma in 2003. Because of concerns for our two growing gems under our care, we also sold our home in Central Islip in August 2003 and moved to our new home in Holbrook a few miles away.

The company was acquired by a billion-dollar company in 2004 and together with another acquisition they were run as one. In July of 2006 the General Manager, Mark challenged me to become a leader for change. Mark was a very charismatic man who was respectful to all and highly regarded by all his employees. He was a real Leader by all definitions of the word and knew how to handle people at all levels.

I accepted the challenge, and was immediately sent to learn and implement changes in the processes at the company locations in Farmingdale and Ronkonkoma. To give me the tools so that I could do the job with which he had tasked me, Mark sent me to the Milwaukee School of Engineering to complete their 'Lean Leadership Course' and I accepted this challenge with gusto.

Now, since 2008, I am the CI Manager and also the Environment Health & Safety Manager at this company in Long Island, which still challenges and motivates me on a daily basis. The challenges have kept coming and I am getting stronger as the days go by . . . . and that is how it should be.

Jag B Mahadeo

"The significant problems we face cannot be solved at the same level of thinking we were at when we created them."

Albert Einstein

End!

For more information on 'The Heart of the Sun' and other writings which may be published soon, please visit the website at *http://theheartofthesun.com*

At this website you will find the pictures inside this book in full color and normal size along with more pictures posted by the author. For your download, you will also find personal articles, poems, power-point files, pdf files, etc. Please use and acknowledge the source. All materials are copyrighted

Please feel free to leave your feedback, comments, suggestions, ideas, and questions for the author Jag B. Mahadeo and he will respond as soon as possible.